CONTENTS

Introduction

Ch.1 The Early Days   **11**

Negative feelings towards the child   12
Coping with emotions   12
Reactions of others in your life   13
Reactions of siblings   14
Useful contacts   16

Ch.2 The Law and Disability   **18**

The law and disability   18
The Equality Act 2010   18
Definition of 'impairment'   19
Persons with HIV infection, cancer and multiple sclerosis 21
Definition of 'long-term effects'   22
Normal day-to-day activities   23
Specialised activities   26
Disabled children   27
Useful contacts   29

Ch.3 Professionals and Organisations That You and   **31**
Your Child Might be Involved With

Clinical psychologist   31
Communication support worker   31
Dietician   32
Educational psychologist   32
General practitioner (GP)   32
Health visitor (Health Service)   32

Key worker   32
Learning disability nurses   33
Learning support assistant / teaching assistant   33
Named officer   33
Paediatric occupational therapist   34
Paediatrician (Health Service)   34
Paediatric neurologist   34
Physiotherapist   34
Portage home visitor   34
School nurse   35
Social worker (Childrens)   35
Special educational needs co-ordinator (SENCO)   35
Useful contacts   36

Ch.4 Finances-The Benefits System   **43**

Right to maternity leave   43
Statutory Maternity Leave   45
Statutory Maternity Pay (SMP)   45
Early births or you lose your baby   46
If you're not eligible for SMP   46
Statutory Maternity Pay (SMP)   47
Proof you're pregnant   47
Maternity benefits   47
Working Tax Credit   47
Income Support   47
Company maternity schemes   48
Extra leave   48
Parental leave   48
Your parenting leave entitlement   48
Special arrangements   49
Dealing with emergencies   49

4

Paternity leave and pay   50

What is paternity leave?   50

Taking paternity leave   50

Births   50

Adoptions and Surrogacy Arrangements   51

Receiving paternity pay   52

Statutory Paternity Pay   52

Contractual Paternity Pay   52

Other leave options   52

Annual leave   53

Unpaid time off   53

Attending Antenatal or Adoption Appointments   53

Still births and sick babies   54

Agency Workers and paternity rights   54

Employment rights during paternity leave   55

Unfair treatment during, or because of, paternity leave   55

Shared parental leave and pay   56

Who can apply for Shared Parental Leave?   57

Shared Parental Pay   58

How to apply for leave and pay   59

New entitlement to Parental Bereavement Leave and Pay   61

Who will be entitled?   61

How can the leave and pay be taken?   62

What notices will be required?   62

What will the evidence requirements be?   63

Adoption leave and pay   63

Other benefits available if your child is disabled   56

Disability Living Allowance/Personal Independence Payment 66

Child Benefit and Child Tax Credit   67

Carer's Allowance   68

Employment and Support Allowance (ESA)   68
Direct Payments (DP)   68
Disabled Facilities Grant   69
Housing Benefit and Council Tax Reduction   69
Family Fund   70
Help with health costs   70
Useful Contacts   72

Ch.5 Education   **74**

Education and the law   74
Reasonable adjustments   74
Portage   74
Special Educational Needs (SEN)   74
Higher education   75
Children with special educational needs (SEN)   76
Support a child can receive   76
Independent support for children of all ages   76
Extra help   76
Requesting an EHC assessment   77
Personal budgets   77
Disabled people and financing studies   79
Students and means tested benefits   81
Useful contacts   83

**Ch.6 Help With Transport and Equipment for You and   84
Your Disabled Child**

Welfare benefits   84
The Blue Badge Scheme   74
The Motability Scheme   86
Use of Public Transport   88
Travel permits for buses and trains   88

6

Help with taxi fares 88
Community transport schemes 89
Equipment available for disabled children-Equipment - 89
provision through local authorities & direct payments
Direct payments 89
Arranging an assessment 90
Wheelchairs 90
Other needs such as nappies and incontinence pads 92
Adaptations to your housing-Disabled Facilities Grants 92
Useful contacts 93

Ch.7 Holidays and Breaks for Disabled Children and **94**
Their Families

Respite breaks or short term breaks 94
Family Based Respite Care 95
Residential Respite Care 96
Play schemes and After School Clubs 96
Respite Care or Short-term Breaks in Your Home 97
Holidays 97
Useful contacts 97

Ch. 8 Disability and Employment **106**

Entering employment 106
Jobcentre plus and Disability Employment Advisors 106
Work programmes 106
Community Work Placement Programme 107
Work Choice 107
Access to Work 108
Training 109
Benefits while training 110
When a person is in work 110

Disability and employers responsibilities 110
Reasonable adjustments in the workplace 110
Recruitment 112
Redundancy and retirement 113
Useful contacts 114

Index

Appendix 1. An overview of welfare benefits

Introduction

Many parents of disabled children find the experience of looking after that child all the more difficult and traumatic because of the lack of information from the professionals who work in the field of disability. In addition to the initial trauma of finding that their child has been diagnosed as disabled, if a diagnosis has been made at all, parents can also be rendered powerless by a lack of information about their child's condition and the ongoing support that they need, plus knowledge of the services, support and benefits to which their child is entitled.

It is hoped that his book, updated to **2019,** will greatly assist the parent(s) of a disabled child and also help to empower and point them in the right direction, enabling people to obtain the support and advice that is needed, both in the early years and later in life.

This book doesn't give information on specific disabilities. This information can be obtained from various sources, such as MENCAP and local libraries, which have a lot of information concerning organisations that exist to provide advice and support. A particularly good organisation is Contact a Family www.contact.org.uk which exists to help parents with disabled children and has a wealth of information. The book is aimed primarily at parent(s) but may be of interest to others such as professionals and agencies, and takes a very practical approach, dealing initially with a discussion of the early days, or months, after having a child diagnosed as disabled. The law and disability is then outlined, along with the professionals involved in the field of disability, and what they do and also the benefit system. Education is discussed, access to education and the responsibilities of local authorities. Holidays and breaks for disabled children and their parents are covered along with transport generally.

This book is a companion volume to A Straightforward Guide To The Rights of Disabled People, which covers the rights of adults who are disabled, either from birth or through accident. I hope it helps a great deal in your journey and makes life easier for both parent and child.

The book opens with a discussion of initial reactions and emotions of parents on learning that their child has a disability. This is a very important time and helps to set the book in context.

Doreen Jarrett

****

Chapter 1

The Early Days

When you have a child with a disability, you will have to cope with a number of issues. On one hand you will have to find your way through the maze of organisations that exist to help you as well as coping with your own emotions and the reactions of relatives and friends plus the reactions of siblings.

Some parents are given the news that their child has a disability at birth, or even before birth. Others might receive the diagnosis after months or years have elapsed. This very much depends on the particular condition. Depending on when you learn of a child's disability, your feelings will vary in reaction and also in intensity. These emotions will cover a whole range of feelings such as anger and disbelief, denial, frustration and guilt. Blame can be placed on oneself or one's partner, which is natural and should eventually pass as it can be rationalised over time. A certain amount of grief will be felt as, although you haven't lost the child you did not have the child that you expected. Ultimately, you will need to change the expectations that you had for him or her. Finally though, comes acceptance and the realisation that you need to live with the situation, love the child and give it the best that you can.

Depression is a common emotion, and can express itself through feelings of pessimism and hopelessness and lead to other difficulties such as problems with eating and sleeping. If you think that you are suffering from depression and recognise the signs then you will need to see your GP, and also in turn health visitors or other agencies.

As mentioned, for some parent's the actual diagnosis of a child's condition cannot be made until after a few years because certain things don't become evident until time has elapsed. This at least gives a parent time to adjust to what might be needed although it in no way diminishes the initial feelings of shock and anger.

Negative feelings towards the child

One of the emotions that you may find particularly difficult to deal with is that of harbouring negative feelings towards your child. The child may look different to others, although this is not always the case. It may take a time to develop a bond and love the child properly. This is perfectly normal and nothing to be ashamed of.

You may also feel over-protective which is a perfectly normal reaction. It can become problematic, however, if being over-protective prevents the child from attaining his or her own independence.

If you have feelings of wanting to harm your child then you will need to seek help immediately. Again, help can be obtained from various sources, such as your GP, health visitor or from a range of agencies detailed at the back of this book. Organisations such as Familylives, CRY-SIS and the NSPCC are particularly useful as they have a lot of experience in this area.

Coping with emotions

With time, and a lot of support, the vast majority of parent's do cope with their situation. They also grow to love their child and get a lot of pleasure from him or her. In the early days (months-years) the best way to cope with feelings that will inevitably arise from the discovery that your child has a disability is to be as open as possible and discuss your feelings with your partner, relatives and friends and also sympathetic professionals. As time goes by you will develop relations with professionals, those who you feel the most empathy with.

There are numerous groups dealing with all sorts of disabilities and they have networks of people who have been through the experience and can share their own experiences with you. You won't feel alone and can learn an awful lot.

It is also very important indeed to attempt to continue as normal a life as possible, going out to see friends for example. Doing the things that you enjoy and providing continuity in your own life is very important indeed and can provide balance.

Reactions of others in your life

Finally, in addition to coping yourself, you need to take into account the feelings of your own partner, if you have a partner or spouse, and ensure that you speak very openly and try to get along together on the same wavelength. Bottling up feelings is very unhealthy and can lead to problems. Relationships between parent's is one of the most important factors in how a family adjusts to disability and how family life develops.

If your partner is male and he is the father of the child, it is highly likely that he will experience the disability in a more negative way, in the first instance. Generally speaking, a mother will bond with a child more quickly than the father may and the father could experience feelings of rejection towards the child. Taking this into account, it is important that both parent's are fully involved with the child and it's development right from the outset, sharing care, appointments with professionals and overall responsibility for development of the child.

Relatives can also exhibit differing emotions, such as guilt (for example, have they been indirectly responsible because of a genetic problem?). It might be that elder relatives, such as grandparents, have an old fashioned view of disability and may need updating with information about the child's condition.

Relatives might want to help in areas such as babysitting and doing housework, and this will involve them more and also take some of the pressure of you.

There is also the question of reactions of friends. Hopefully, your friends will react positively and want to help. It is important, once again, to be as open as possible. Allow them to see the baby as soon as possible which will reinforce the fact that the baby is a person rather than a disability. Friends can also offer practical support, particularly if they are good friends and are intelligent and sympathetic.

Reactions of siblings

If you have children, it is important to tell them about the child's disability as soon as possible. This goes without saying. How much you tell your children will depend on how old they are. Generally, children under a certain age, say 3 years old, are still too young to understand details about the disability or condition of their sibling. They can, however, be told that you are feeling sad and that their new baby sister or brother needs a lot of care and attention.

Older children can be told a little more about their sibling's disability. Use simple terms and try not to confuse them. Most children, older children, will understand. It is important to remember that you will still need to divide your time equally between children so as not to exclude them. Above all, try to involve sibling's in the child's development.

Coping with disability, and the reactions to disability, and the attendant emotions, is not easy. However, very importantly, try to remember that you are not alone and that there are numerous support groups out there with a network of people who are only to willing to offer support and share their experiences.

In the next chapter, we will look at how the law impacts on disability. Although this is a dry area, it is important to understand as it will give you an idea of your rights and the child's rights.

****

Useful Contacts

KIDS is a leading disabled children's charity that has been in existence for over 40 years working to enable disabled children and young people and their families www.kids.org.uk

Disability Rights (Main campaigning group)
Plexal
14 East Bay Lane
Here East
Queen Elizabeth Olympic Park
Stratford
London
E20 3BS
www.disabilityrightsuk.org
Office Number: 0330 995 0400
This line is not an advice line.

There are advice lines which can be accessed on the website

Child Disability help (general sites)
www.scope.org.uk/support/families/parents/help
www.gov.uk/help-for-disabled-chil

Contact a family (contact for families with disabled children)
209-211 City Road
London EC1V 1JN
0208 7608 8700
Helpline 0808 808 3555
www.contact.org.uk/

MENCAP (mental health charity)

The Royal MENCAP Society is a registered charity that offers services to children, young people and adults with learning disabilities. It offers help and advice on benefits, housing and employment. It also offers help and advice to anyone with any other issues, or will direct them to the right place. It can also provide information and support for leisure, recreational services (Gateway Clubs), residential services and holidays.

0808 808 1111

www.mencap.org

Familylives (support for families)

www.familylives.org.uk

0808 800 2222

CRY-SIS (helps with sleepless nights/support group)

www.cry-sis.org.uk

08451 228 669

****

Chapter 2

The Law and Disability

Although this book is specifically about the rights of disabled children, those rights sit within the wider body of law that covers all people with disabilities. Below is an outline of the law generally as it impacts on disability. This will help to set the scene and create a knowledge base from which you can develop your understanding.

The law and disability

In general, the wide body of laws that protect all people in the United Kingdom will apply to disabled people. Such laws can include consumer law, employment law and family law. However, in certain important respects, the law that applies to disabled people, and gives an extra layer of protection is the Equality Act 2010. This law is wide ranging and incorporated many previous Acts, such as the Disability Discrimination Act, and also clearly defines discrimination. Below is a summary of the Act. However, as we go through the book continuous reference will be made to the Act as it applies to the many areas of life, such as employment and transport, that directly affects disabled people.

The Equality Act 2010

The Equality Act 2010 prohibits discrimination against people with the protected characteristics that are specified in section 4 of the Act. Disability is one of the specified protected characteristics. Protection from discrimination for disabled people applies to disabled people in a range of circumstances, covering the provision of goods, facilities and services, the exercise of public functions, premises, work, education, and associations. Only those people who are defined as disabled in accordance with section 6 of the Act, and the associated Schedules and regulations made under that section, will be entitled to the protection that the Act provides to disabled people. However, importantly, the Act also provides protection for non-disabled people who are subjected to direct discrimination or harassment because of their association with a disabled person or because they are wrongly perceived to be disabled.

The Act defines a disabled person as, simply, a person with a disability. A person has a disability for the purposes of the Act if he or she has a physical or mental impairment and the impairment has a substantial and long-term adverse effect on his or her ability to carry out normal day-to-day activities.

This means that, in general:

o the person must have an impairment that is either physical or mental

o the impairment must have adverse effects which are substantial

o the substantial adverse effects must be long-term and

o the long-term substantial adverse effects must have an effect on normal day-to-day activities

Definition of 'impairment'

The definition requires that the effects which a person may experience must arise from a physical or mental impairment. The term mental or physical impairment should be given its ordinary meaning. It is not necessary for the cause of the impairment to be established, nor does the impairment have to be the result of an illness. In many cases, there will be no dispute as to whether a person has an impairment. Any disagreement is more likely to be about whether the effects of the impairment are sufficient to fall within the definition and in particular whether they are long-term. This is a crucial fact.

Whether a person is disabled for the purposes of the Act is generally determined by reference to the effect that an impairment has on that person's ability to carry out normal day-to-day activities. An exception to this is a person with severe disfigurement. A disability can arise from a wide range of impairments which can be:

- sensory impairments, such as those affecting sight or hearing;

- impairments with fluctuating or recurring effects such as Rheumatoid arthritis, Myalgic encephalitis (ME), Chronic fatigue syndrome (CFS), Fibromyalgia, Depression and Epilepsy;

- progressive, such as Motor neurone disease, Muscular dystrophy, and forms of Dementia;

- auto-immune conditions such as Systemic lupus erythematosis (SLE);

- organ specific, including Respiratory conditions, such as Asthma, and cardiovascular diseases, including Thrombosis, Stroke and Heart disease;

- developmental, such as Autistic spectrum disorders (ASD), Dyslexia and Dyspraxia;

- learning disabilities;

- mental health conditions with symptoms such as anxiety, low mood, panic attacks, phobias, or unshared perceptions;

eating disorders; bipolar affective disorders; obsessive compulsive disorders; personality disorders; post traumatic stress disorder, and some self-harming behaviour;

- o Mental illnesses, such as depression and schizophrenia;
- o produced by injury to the body, including to the brain.

Persons with HIV infection, cancer and multiple sclerosis

The Act states that a person who has cancer, HIV infection or Multiple sclerosis (MS) is a disabled person. This means that the person is protected by the Act effectively from the point of diagnosis.

Certain conditions are not regarded as impairments. These are:

- o addiction to, or dependency on, alcohol, nicotine, or any other substance (other than in consequence of the substance being medically prescribed);
- o the condition known as seasonal allergic rhinitis (e.g. hayfever), except where it aggravates the effect of another condition;
- o tendency to set fires;
- o tendency to steal;
- o tendency to physical or sexual abuse of other persons;
- o exhibitionism;

A person with an excluded condition may nevertheless be protected as a disabled person if he or she has an accompanying impairment which meets the requirements of the definition. For example, a person who is addicted to a substance such as alcohol may also have depression, or a physical impairment such as liver damage, arising from the alcohol addiction. While this person would not meet the

21

definition simply on the basis of having an addiction, he or she may still meet the definition as a result of the effects of the depression or the liver damage.

Disfigurements which consist of a tattoo (which has not been removed), non-medical body piercing, or something attached through such piercing, are treated as not having a substantial adverse effect on the person's ability to carry out normal day-to-day activities.

The Act says that, except for the provisions in Part 12 (Transport) and section 190 (improvements to let dwelling houses), the provisions of the Act also apply in relation to a person who previously has had a disability as defined in the Act. This means that someone who is no longer disabled, but who met the requirements of the definition in the past, will still be covered by the Act. Also protected would be someone who continues to experience debilitating effects as a result of treatment for a past disability.

Definition of 'long-term effects'

The Act states that, for the purpose of deciding whether a person is disabled, a long-term effect of an impairment is one:

o   which has lasted at least 12 months; or

o   where the total period for which it lasts, from the time of the first onset, is likely to be at least 12 months; or

o   which is likely to last for the rest of the life of the person affected

Special provisions apply when determining whether the effects of an impairment that has fluctuating or recurring effects are long-term.

22

Also a person who is deemed to be a disabled person does not need to satisfy the long-term requirement.

The cumulative effect of related impairments should be taken into account when determining whether the person has experienced a long-term effect for the purposes of meeting the definition of a disabled person. The substantial adverse effect of an impairment which has developed from, or is likely to develop from, another impairment should be taken into account when determining whether the effect has lasted, or is likely to last at least twelve months, or for the rest of the life of the person affected.

Normal day-to-day activities

In general, day-to-day activities are things people do on a regular or daily basis, and examples include shopping, reading and writing, having a conversation or using the telephone, watching television, getting washed and dressed, preparing and eating food, carrying out household tasks, walking and travelling by various forms of transport, and taking part in social activities. Normal day-to-day activities can include general work-related activities, and study and education-related activities, such as interacting with colleagues, following instructions, using a computer, driving, carrying out interviews, preparing written documents, and keeping to a timetable or a shift pattern.

The term 'normal day-to-day activities' is not intended to include activities which are normal only for a particular person, or a small group of people. In deciding whether an activity is a normal day-to-day activity, account should be taken of how far it is carried out by people on a daily or frequent basis. In this context, 'normal' should be given its ordinary, everyday meaning.

23

A normal day-to-day activity is not necessarily one that is carried out by a majority of people. For example, it is possible that some activities might be carried out only, or more predominantly, by people of a particular gender, such as breast-feeding or applying make-up, and cannot therefore be said to be normal for most people. They would nevertheless be considered to be normal day-to-day activities.

Also, whether an activity is a normal day-to-day activity should not be determined by whether it is more normal for it to be carried out at a particular time of day. For example, getting out of bed and getting dressed are activities that are normally associated with the morning. They may be carried out much later in the day by workers who work night shifts, but they would still be considered to be normal day-to-day activities. The following examples demonstrate a range of day-to-day effects on impairment:

o   Difficulty in getting dressed,
o   Difficulty carrying out activities associated with toileting, or caused by frequent minor incontinence;
o   Difficulty preparing a meal,
o   Difficulty eating;
o   Difficulty going out of doors unaccompanied, for example, because the person has a phobia, a physical restriction, or a learning disability;
o   Difficulty waiting or queuing,
o   Difficulty using transport; for example, because of physical restrictions, pain or fatigue, a frequent need for a lavatory or as a result of a mental impairment or learning disability;
o   Difficulty in going up or down steps, stairs or gradients;
o   A total inability to walk, or an ability to walk only a short distance without difficulty;

o Difficulty entering or staying in environments that the person perceives as strange or frightening;

o Behaviour which challenges people around the person, making it difficult for the person to be accepted in public places;

o Persistent difficulty crossing a road safely,

o Persistent general low motivation or loss of interest in everyday activities;

o Difficulty accessing and moving around buildings;

o Difficulty operating a computer, for example, because of physical restrictions in using a keyboard, a visual impairment or a learning disability;

o Difficulty picking up and carrying objects of moderate weight, such as a bag of shopping or a small piece of luggage, with one hand;

o Inability to converse, or give instructions orally, in the person's native spoken language;

o Difficulty understanding or following simple verbal instructions;

o Difficulty hearing and understanding another person speaking clearly over the voice telephone

o Persistent and significant difficulty in reading or understanding written material where this is in the person's native written language,

o Frequent confused behaviour, intrusive thoughts, feelings of being controlled, or delusions;

o Persistently wanting to avoid people or significant difficulty taking part in normal social interaction or forming social relationships, o Persistent difficulty in recognising, or remembering the names of, familiar people such as family or friends;

o Persistent distractibility or difficulty concentrating;

o Compulsive activities or behaviour, or difficulty in adapting after a reasonable period to minor changes in a routine.

Whether a person satisfies the definition of a disabled person for the purposes of the Act will depend upon the full circumstances of the case. That is, whether the substantial adverse effect of the impairment on normal day-to-day activities is long term.

Specialised activities

Where activities are themselves highly specialised or involve highly specialised levels of attainment, they would not be regarded as normal day-to-day activities for most people. In some instances work-related activities are so highly specialised that they would not be regarded as normal day-to-day activities. The same is true of other specialised activities such as playing a musical instrument to a high standard of achievement; taking part in activities where very specific skills or level of ability are required; or playing a particular sport to a high level of ability, such as would be required for a professional footballer or athlete. Where activities involve highly specialised skills or levels of attainment, they would not be regarded as normal day-to-day activities for most people.

Normal day-to-day activities also include activities that are required to maintain personal well-being or to ensure personal safety, or the safety of other people. Account should be taken of whether the effects of an impairment have an impact on whether the person is inclined to carry out or neglect basic functions such as

26

eating, drinking, sleeping, keeping warm or personal hygiene; or to exhibit behaviour which puts the person or other people at risk.

Indirect effects

An impairment may not directly prevent someone from carrying out one or more normal day-to-day activities, but it may still have a substantial adverse effect on how the person carries out those activities. For example pain or fatigue: where an impairment causes pain or fatigue, the person may have the ability to carry out a normal day-to-day activity, but may be restricted in the way that it is carried out because of experiencing pain in doing so. Or the impairment might make the activity more than usually fatiguing so that the person might not be able to repeat the task over a sustained period of time.

Disabled children

The effects of impairments may not be apparent in babies and young children because they are too young to have developed the ability to carry out activities that are normal for older children and adults. Regulations provide that an impairment to a child under six years old is to be treated as having a substantial and long-term adverse effect on the ability of that child to carry out normal day-to-day activities where it would normally have a substantial and long-term adverse effect on the ability of a person aged six years or over to carry out normal day-to-day activities.

Children aged six and older are subject to the normal requirements of the definition. That is, that they must have an impairment which has a substantial and long-term adverse effect on their ability to carry out normal day-to-day activities. However, in considering the ability of a child aged six or over to carry out a normal day-to-day activity, it is necessary to take account of the level of achievement which would be normal for a person of a similar age.

Part 6 of the Act provides protection for disabled pupils and students by preventing discrimination against them at school or in post-16 education because of, or for a reason related to, their disability. A pupil or student must satisfy the definition of disability as described in this guidance in order to be protected by Part 6 of the Act. The duties for schools in the Act, including the duty for schools to make reasonable adjustments for disabled children, are designed to dovetail with duties under the Special Educational Needs (SEN) framework which are based on a separate definition of special educational needs. Further information on these duties can be found in the SEN Code of Practice and the Equality and Human Rights Commission's Codes of

****

Useful Contacts

Gov.uk

www.gov.uk/rights-disabled-person/overview

Children's Legal Centre Head Office)

Coram Children's Legal Centre
Riverside Office Centre
Century House North
North Station Road
COLCHESTER
CO1 1RE
Tel: 01206 714 650 (*for general queries only, they cannot give legal advice or a referral through this number*)
Fax: 01206 714 660
E-mail: info@coramclc.org.uk

London Office

Coram Children's Legal Centre
Coram Campus
41 Brunswick Square
LONDON
WC1N 1AZ
Tel: 020 7713 0089 (*for general queries only, they cannot give legal advice or a referral through this number*)

Disability Law Service

39-45 Cavell Street
The Foundry
17 Oval way, London, SE11 5RR
0207 791 9800
www.dls.org.uk

Disability Rights Commission

Telephone: 08457 622 633

Textphone: 08457 622 644

You can speak to an operator at any time between 8am and 8pm, Monday to Friday.

Fax: 08457 778 878

Post: DRC Helpline

FREEPOST MID02164

Stratford upon Avon

CV37 9BR

Disability Rights UK

Plexal

14 East Bay Lane

Here East

Queen Elizabeth Olympic Park

Stratford

London

E20 3BS

www.disabilityrightsuk.org

Office Number: 0330 995 0400

This line is not an advice line.

There are advice lines which can be accessed on the website

****

Chapter 3

Professionals and Organisations That You and Your Child Might be Involved With

---

When you have a disabled child, you will inevitably come into contact with a variety of different professionals from health services, social services, education and different voluntary organisations. This will continue throughout your son or daughter's childhood and early adulthood, sometimes throughout his or her life.

This can be overwhelming and in the first instance you may be confused about each persons role, how they can help you and who employs them. This chapter outlines the different roles that professionals play and how they can help you. In addition, there are a number of agencies listed where you can get all the advice and support that you need. Some of these agencies are statutory, which are the ones run by the state under legislation, such as the NHS, and some are voluntary. The one common denominator is that they all provide invaluable help and support.

People who may be involved in your childs care.

Clinical psychologist

A clinical psychologist is a health professional who helps people with specific problems with learning or behaviour difficulties.

Communication support worker

A communication support worker works alongside teachers to provide sign language support for young deaf children in nursery or school.

Dietician

A dietician is a health professional who gives advice about nutrition and swallowing or feeding difficulties.

Educational psychologist

An educational psychologist is qualified teacher who is also trained as a psychologist. They help children who find it difficult to learn or to understand or communicate with others. They can assess your child's development and provide support and advice.

General practitioner (GP)

A GP is a family doctor who works in a surgery either on their own or with other GPs. Your doctor deals with your child's general health and can refer you to clinics, hospitals and specialists when needed.

Health visitor (Health Service)

A health visitor is a registered nurse or a midwife with additional training. They visit families at home to give help, advice and practical assistance about the care of very young children. Some areas have specialist health visitors who have particular experience and expertise supporting families with a young disabled child.

Key worker

Some families have a key worker. A key worker will see you regularly and make sure you have all the information you need. They will also make sure that services from all the different areas, including health, education and social services, are well co-ordinated.

Key workers can act as a central point of contact for professionals working with your family, and make sure information about your child is shared where necessary.

'Designated' and 'non-designated' key workers

A 'non-designated' key worker is someone who is already working with a family, in another role. They take on the responsibilities of a key worker in addition to any other help or therapy they provide for the child or parents. 'Designated' key workers are employed mainly to co-ordinate information and support for families.

Learning disability nurses

Learning disability nurses are specialist nurses who work with children and adults with a learning disability and with their families. They can help you find services for your child.

Learning support assistant / teaching assistant

A learning support assistant or teaching assistant is someone who works alongside teachers. They support individual children or small groups to help them learn and take part in activities in schools or nurseries.

Named officer

A named officer is your family's contact person at the local education authority, if it issues a statement of special educational needs for your child. They manage your child's statutory assessment and write up the statement of needs.

*

Paediatric occupational therapist

A paediatric occupational therapist helps children with difficulties in carrying out the activities of everyday life, such as sitting in a chair, holding a spoon and fork or drinking from a cup. They carry out assessments to see if your child would benefit from using specialist equipment like adapted cups, buggies or chairs. They can also advise you on lifting and handling your child safely.

Paediatrician (Health Service)

A paediatrician is a doctor who specialises in working with babies and children. They are often the first point of contact for families who find out their child has an impairment or medical condition. Paediatricians may give you a diagnosis about your child's condition, answer any questions you may have and refer you to specialist services.

Paediatric neurologist

A paediatric neurologist is a doctor who specialises in how the brain works in very young children.

Physiotherapist

A physiotherapist is a health professional who specialises in physical and motor development. They can assess your child and develop a plan that might include helping your child control their head movement, sit, crawl or walk. A physiotherapist may see your child at home or in other settings, like a nursery.

Portage home visitor

An eucational professional who can come to the home of pre-school children with special educational needs and their families. Portage home visitors can come from a range of professional backgrounds. They may be teachers, therapists, nursery nurses, health visitors or volunteers with relevant experience.

School nurse

A school nurse is a medical nurse, based in a school, who provides support for children's medical needs.

Social worker (Childrens)

A social worker is a professional who provides practical help and advice about counselling, transport, home help and other services. They are normally employed by the local council. Social workers may also be able to help you with claiming benefits or getting equipment you need at home.

Special educational needs co-ordinator (SENCO)

SENCOs are members of staff at a nursery, playgroup or school who co-ordinate special educational needs activities and services. They make sure that children who have special educational needs receive appropriate support.

****

Useful contacts

Support organisations

There are numerous support organisations that exist to help parents with disabled children. The internet has many useful sites which can direct you to specific organisations. One particulalry good site is http://www.accessiblecountryside.org.uk/organisations. They have a comprehensive list which is very helpful and detailed. Below are listed a few such organisations.

Cerebra

A unique charity set up to help improve the lives of children and young people with brain- related conditions through researching, educating and directly supporting children and their carers.

2nd Floor Offices
The Lyric Buildings
King Street
Carmarthen
SA31 1BD
Telephone: +44 (0) 1267 244200
Fax: +44 (0) 1267 244201
Email: enquiries@cerebra.org.uk

Parent Support
Freepost Address Cerebra (Parent Support)
FREEPOST SWC3360
Carmarthen
SA31 1ZY
Email: info@cerebra.org.uk
Helpline (freephone): 0800 328 1159

Citizens Advice Bureau

Helps people resolve their legal, money and other problems by providing free, confidential and impartial information and advice. It has a number of field offices across England. Myddelton House,

Citizens Advice,
3rd Floor North,
200 Aldersgate, London,
EC1A 4HD
www.citizensadvice.org.uk (local offices)
www.adviceguide.org.uk

Contact a Family

A UK-wide charity providing support, advice and information for families with children with additional needs. It runs a helpline for family members and can help you get in touch with other parents of disabled children living near you. Will divert calls to Scotland, Northern Ireland and Wales as appropriate

www.contact.org.uk
808 8083555

Council for Disabled Children

A national forum for the discussion, development and dissemination of a wide range of policy and practice issues relating to service provision for children and young people with disabilities and special educational needs. Membership is drawn from a wide range of professional, voluntary and statutory organisations and includes parent representatives and representatives of disabled people.

WeWork,
115 Mare Street,
London E8 4RU
London
EC1V 7QE
www.councilfordisabledchildren.org.uk
0808 8083555

Family and Childcare Trust

A national childcare charity working to promote high-quality, affordable childcare for everyone. It provides information about all aspects of childcare.
2nd Floor, The Bridge
73-81 Southwark Bridge Road
London
SE1 0NQ
www.familyandchildcaretrust.org
020 79407510 (admin only)

Department for Education

The Department for Education is responsible for education and children's services in England. We work to achieve a highly educated society in which opportunity is equal for children and young people, no matter what their background or family circumstances. DfE is a ministerial department, supported by 9 agencies and public bodies.

https://www.gov.uk/government/organisations/department-for-education
0370 000 2288

Disability Rights UK

Plexal

14 East Bay Lane

Here East

Queen Elizabeth Olympic Park

Stratford

London

E20 3BS

www.disabilityrightsuk.org

Office Number: 0330 995 0400

This line is not an advice line.

There are advice lines which can be accessed on the website

Family Information Service (FIS)

The FIS can give you information about the full range of childcare and other services for children, young people and families available in the area. You can contact the FIS through your local authority office or find you local FIS contact details at the following website. www.daycaretrust.org.uk/findyourFIS

Information Advice and Support Services Network (IASSN)

The Information, Advice and Support Services Network (IASS Network) provide training and support to local Information Advice and Support (IAS) Services across England. The IASS Network was previously known as the National Parent Partnership Network (NPPN), who undertook a similar role with local Parent Partnership Services. www.councilfordisabledchildren.org.uk

Mencap

The Royal MENCAP Society is a registered charity that offers services to children, young people and adults with learning disabilities. It offers help and advice on benefits, housing and employment. It also offers help and advice to anyone with any other issues, or will direct them to the right place. It can also provide information and support for leisure, recreational services (Gateway Clubs), residential services and holidays.

www.mencap.org.uk
help@mencap.org.uk
0808 8081111

NHS Direct

A 24-hour nurse advice and health information service, providing confidential information on what to do if you or a family member is feeling ill, have particular health conditions, or need local healthcare services or self-help and support organisations.
www.nhsdirect.nhs.uk
0300 311 22 33
Email: england.contactus@nhs.net

The Royal National Institute of Blind People (RNIB)

RNIB is the leading charity offering information, support and advice to almost two million people with sight loss. It has practical ways to help those living with sight loss, including advice about travelling, shopping, managing money and finances, and technology for blind and partially sighted people.

105 Judd Street

London

WC1H 9NE

www.rnib.org.uk

helpline@rnib.org.uk

0303 1239999

Scope

Scope is the UK's leading disability charity. Its focus is on children, young people and adults with cerebral palsy and people living with other severe and complex impairments. Its vision is a world where disabled people have the same opportunities to fulfill their life ambitions as non-disabled people.

www.scope.org.uk

0808 800 3333

Sense

The major UK voluntary organisation for children, young people and adults born with multi- sensory impairment (MSI) and their families. The website has information about the help and services available to people with MSI, their families and professionals.

101 Pentonville Road

London N1 9LG

www.sense.org.uk

info@sense.org.uk

0300 330 9520

Transition Information Network (TIN)

The network is hosted by the Council for Disabled Children. The aim of the website is to provide information to parents and practitioners about disabled young people's transition to adulthood. There is also a young people's section with information, news and events.

43 Fore Street,
Totnes,
TQ9 5HN,
UK
www.transitioninfonetwork.org.uk

Telephone: +44 (0)1803 865 669

****

Chapter 4
Finances-The Benefits System

Having looked at the role of the professional, in this chapter we will look at the rights of the disabled child and the rights of their parents in relation to the benefit system. The whole range of welfare benefits available and also entitlements is contained within Appendix 1. However, for the purposes of this chapter we will start with the period of pregnancy. Pregnancy and maternity is now one of the protected characteristics in the Equality Act 2010 and there is implied into every woman's term of employment a maternity equality clause (s 73 Equality Act 2010). The Act protects women from direct discrimination (s 13(1)) and indirect discrimination (s 19(1)) in relation to pregnancy and maternity.

Right to maternity leave

When you take time off to have a baby you might be eligible for:

- Statutory Maternity Leave
- Statutory Maternity Pay
- paid time off for antenatal care
- extra help from the government

You may also be eligible to get Shared Parental Leave and Pay.

Employment rights when on leave

Your employment rights are protected while on Statutory Maternity Leave. This includes your right to:

- pay rises
- build up (accrue) holiday
- return to work

Leave

Statutory Maternity Leave is 52 weeks. It's made up of:

- Ordinary Maternity Leave - first 26 weeks
- Additional Maternity Leave - last 26 weeks

You don't have to take 52 weeks but you must take 2 weeks' leave after your baby is born (or 4 weeks if you work in a factory). You may be entitled to take some of your leave as Shared Parental Leave.

Start date and early births

Usually, the earliest you can start your leave is 11 weeks before the expected week of childbirth. Leave will also start:

- the day after the birth if the baby is early
- automatically if you're off work for a pregnancy-related illness in the 4 weeks before the week (Sunday to Saturday) that your baby is due

Change your date for returning to work

You must give your employer at least 8 weeks' notice if you want to change your return to work date.

Pay

Statutory Maternity Pay (SMP) is paid for up to 39 weeks. You get:

- 90% of your average weekly earnings (before tax) for the first 6 weeks

- £145.18 or 90% of your average weekly earnings (whichever is lower) for the next 33 weeks

SMP is paid in the same way as your wages (for example monthly or weekly). Tax and National Insurance will be deducted.

If you take Shared Parental Leave you'll get Statutory Shared Parental Pay (ShPP). ShPP is £145.18 a week or 90% of your average weekly earnings, whichever is lower.

Start date

SMP usually starts when you take your maternity leave. It starts automatically if you're off work for a pregnancy-related illness in the 4 weeks before the week (Sunday to Saturday) that your baby is due.

Statutory Maternity Leave

You qualify for Statutory Maternity Leave if:

- you're an employee not a 'worker'
- you give your employer the correct notice

It doesn't matter how long you've been with your employer, how many hours you work or how much you get paid.

You can't get Statutory Maternity Leave if you have a child through surrogacy - you could get Statutory Adoption Leave and Pay instead.

Statutory Maternity Pay (SMP)

To qualify for SMP you must:

- earn on average at least £116 a week
- give the correct notice

- give proof you're pregnant
- have worked for your employer continuously for at least 26 weeks continuing into the 'qualifying week' - the 15th week before the expected week of childbirth

You can't get SMP if you go into police custody during your maternity pay period. It won't restart when you're discharged.

Early births or you lose your baby

You can still get Statutory Maternity Leave and SMP if your baby:

- is born early
-]is stillborn after the start of your 24th week of pregnancy
- dies after being born

If you're not eligible for SMP

Your employer must give you form SMP1 explaining why you can't get SMP within 7 days of making their decision. You may be eligible for Maternity Allowance instead.

How to claim

Statutory Maternity Leave

At least 15 weeks before your due date, tell your employer when the baby is due and when you want to start your maternity leave. Your employer can ask for this in writing.

Your employer must write to you within 28 days confirming your start and end dates.

Use the maternity planner to work out when you must claim your maternity leave.

Statutory Maternity Pay (SMP)

Tell your employer you want to stop work to have a baby and the day you want your SMP to start. You must give them at least 28 days' notice (in writing if they ask for it) and proof that you're pregnant. Your employer must confirm within 28 days how much SMP you'll get and when it will start and stop. If they decide you're not eligible, they must give you form SMP1 within 7 days of making their decision and explain why.

Proof you're pregnant

You need to give your employer proof of the pregnancy to get SMP. You don't need it for maternity leave. Within 21 days of your SMP start date (or as soon as possible if the baby's born early) give your employer either:

- a letter from your doctor or midwife
- your MATB1 certificate - doctors and midwives will give you this no more than 20 weeks before the due date

You won't get SMP if you don't give your employer proof that the baby is due.

Maternity benefits

Working Tax Credit - this can continue for 39 weeks after you go on maternity leave

Income Support - you may get this while you're not working

You could get a £500 Sure Start Maternity Grant (usually if it's your first child).

If you're not eligible for Statutory Maternity Pay, you could get Maternity Allowance from the government.

Company maternity schemes

You might get more than the statutory amount of leave and pay if your employer has a company maternity scheme. They can't offer you less than the statutory amount.

Extra leave

You could get 18 weeks' unpaid parental leave after the birth - this may be restricted to 4 weeks per year.

Parental leave

Parental leave is a legal right to take time off from work to look after a child or make arrangements for a child's welfare. Employers are not legally required to pay workers taking parental leave, so many do not. However, if you are on a low income, you may qualify for income support while you are on parental leave.

Mothers and fathers qualify for statutory parental leave whether they are biological or adoptive parents.

Parental leave is different to other parenting-related leave arrangements such as maternity, adoption and paternity leave.

Your parenting leave entitlement

Working parents are entitled to take up to 18 weeks' parental leave per child up to their eighteenth birthday. Parental leave can be taken for any reason as long as it's related to the care of your child. Examples of the way it might be used include:
- spending more time with your child in their early years;
- accompanying your child during a stay in hospital;
- looking at new schools;

- settling your child into new childcare arrangements;

- enabling your family to spend more time together. For example, taking them to stay with grandparents.

If you take less than four weeks' parental leave in one block, you have the legal right to return to your old job. If you take more than four weeks in a block, you are only entitled to return to the job you did before if it is reasonably practicable. If it isn't, your employer must give you a comparable and appropriate job.

You can only take parental leave if you have been continuously employed for not less than a year and have, or expect to have responsibility for the child.

"Responsibility for the child" is a legal term. You will normally have responsibility for the child if you are the mother of the child or the father of the child and you are either married to the mother of the child or your name appears on the birth certificate of the child, having registered jointly with the mother.

Special arrangements

Some employers allow flexibility in the way parental leave is taken. You might, therefore, be able to work reduced hours over a given period, for example, without losing any pay. Or your employer may allow you parental leave even though your child is over the statutory age for you to legally qualify.

Dealing with emergencies

Even if you don't qualify for parental leave, you should be able to get time off to deal with genuine emergencies. You have the right to take a reasonable amount of unpaid time off to deal with certain emergencies involving people you care for. You qualify for "time off for dependents" regardless of how long you have been working for your employer.

Paternity leave and pay

Employees whose partner is having a baby, adopting a child or having a baby through a surrogacy arrangement may be entitled to paternity leave and pay. Workers, while not entitled to paternity leave, may be entitled to receive paternity pay.

What is paternity leave?

Paternity leave is a period of either one or two consecutive weeks that fathers or partners can take off from work to care for their baby or child. It is available to employees who:

- have or expect to have responsibility for the child's upbringing

- are the biological father of the child, the mother's husband or partner (including same sex relationships) **or** the partner of the primary adopter

- have worked continuously for their employer for 26 weeks ending with the 15th week before the baby is due, or the end of the week in which the child's adopter is notified of being matched with the child (UK adoption), or the date the child enters the UK (overseas adoptions).

Taking paternity leave
Births

An employee must inform their employer no later than the end of the 15th week before the expected week of childbirth that they wish to take paternity leave. They should say when the baby is due, if they're going to take one or two weeks off, and when they expect their paternity leave to start.

An employee can choose for their leave to begin on:

- the day the baby is born
- a certain number of days after the baby is born
- a specific date which is not earlier than when the baby is due.

Paternity leave cannot start before the baby is born and the baby may not arrive on time. An employer should therefore be prepared to flexible with cover arrangements for employees planning to take paternity leave.

Employees will need to complete their paternity leave within 56 days of the actual date of birth of the child.

Adoptions and Surrogacy Arrangements

When adopting, one partner, if they qualify, can take adoption leave as the main adopter and the other may be entitled to paternity leave.

A period of paternity leave when adopting a child can start:

- on the date of placement
- an agreed number of days after the date of placement
- on the date the child arrives in the UK or an agreed number of days after (for overseas adoption)
- the day the child is born or the day after for surrogate parents.

In all adoptions, an employee will need to have taken their Paternity Leave within 56 days of the placement date.

Receiving paternity pay

Employees or workers who take time off may be entitled to either Statutory Paternity Pay or Contractual Paternity Pay.

Statutory Paternity Pay

Statutory Paternity Pay will be payable if an employee or worker has been:

• working continuously for one company for at least 26 weeks ending with the 15th week before the expected week of childbirth

• has an average weekly earnings at least equal to the lower earnings limit for National Insurance contributions.

Since April 2018 the rate has been £145.18 per week or 90 per cent of the average weekly earnings, whichever is less.

Contractual Paternity Pay

An employer may choose to offer a rate of pay which is higher than the statutory rate. The amount and the length for which it is paid should be set out in the terms and conditions of employment. Contractual paternity pay cannot be lower than the statutory rate.

Other leave options

An employee may not qualify for paternity leave, or they may want to take some additional time off when the baby is born. In these circumstances an employee could consider the following:

Shared Parental Leave

Give parents more flexibility in how they share the care of their child in the first year following birth or adoption. Eligible parents can exchange part of their maternity or adoption leave for Shared Parental Leave. They can then share this leave with each other in a way that best suit their needs in caring for their child.

Annual leave

An employee could submit an annual leave request to take time off at the time the baby is born. This should be done in accordance with the employer's annual leave policy and the employer would have the right to accept or decline the request depending on business needs.

Unpaid time off

An employee could discuss with their employer whether they could come to an agreement to take unpaid time off. This could only be done if both employee and employer agree to it.

Attending Antenatal or Adoption Appointments

Antenatal classes

Fathers and partners of a pregnant woman are entitled to unpaid time off during working hours to accompany her to two ante-natal appointments. The time off should not exceed 6.5 hours per appointment and should be used to travel to and attend the appointment. If this takes less than 6.5 hours the employee should return to work unless alternative arrangements have been made with their employer.

There is no legal right to paid time off for attending antenatal appointments. However, an employee's contract of employment may entitle them to the time off with pay. If an employee does not want to take unpaid time off, they could request annual leave or ask if they could work the hours at a different time.

The right to two unpaid antenatal appointments also includes employees who will become parents through a surrogacy arrangement if they expect to satisfy the conditions for, and intend to apply for, a Parental Order.

Adoption appointments

The main adopter is able to take paid time off for up to 5 adoption appointments. The main adopter's partner (secondary adopter) is entitled to take unpaid time off for up to 2 appointments.

Still births and sick babies

If the baby is stillborn after the twenty fourth week of pregnancy or if the baby is born alive at any point (even if the baby later passes away) the employee is entitled to full paternity rights if they satisfy the conditions above.

When a baby is born prematurely or with health needs an employee may not want to be thinking about work. An employer should offer appropriate support in these circumstances.

Agency Workers and paternity rights

Agency workers do not usually qualify for paternity leave (unless they are an employee of the agency). However, an agency worker may qualify for paternity pay if they meet the qualifying criteria. If an agency worker qualifies for paternity pay they should write to their agency at least 28 days before they want the payment to begin stating:

- the agency worker's name
- when the baby is due
- when the worker would like the payment to begin
- whether they are requesting one or two weeks pay.

Agency workers can usually choose when to make themselves available for work so may choose to be unavailable for work for a period of time after the baby is born. An agency worker whose partner is pregnant has the right to attend two unpaid antenatal appointments with their partner once they have completed a twelve week qualifying period with one hiring company.

Employment rights during paternity leave

An employee has the right to not be treated less favourably by their employer for taking, or proposing to take, paternity leave. An employee also has the right to return to their own job following a period of paternity leave and their terms and conditions should remain the same.

Annual leave (including Bank Holidays where applicable) continues to accrue during paternity leave and an employee must be able to take this leave at some point during their leave year.

Unfair treatment during, or because of, paternity leave

If an employee feels that they have been treated unfairly because of taking, or proposing to take, paternity leave, they should first consider raising the issue informally. Some issues can be resolved quickly through a conversation with a line manager or other person within the business.

If an informal approach does not work, an employee has the option of raising a formal complaint (also known as a grievance). This should be done in writing and can make the employer aware of how strongly the employee feels about the situation, while also giving the employer the opportunity to resolve it.

As a last resort the employee could consider making a complaint to an Employment Tribunal. There is generally a three month time limit for bringing a claim to Employment Tribunal. However this time limit can be paused if Early Conciliation is taking place.

Shared parental leave and pay

Shared Parental Leave (SPL) enables eligible mothers, fathers, partners and adopters to choose how to share time off work after their child is born or placed for adoption. This could involve returning to work for part of the time and then resuming leave at a later date.

How Shared Parental Leave works

Shared Parental Leave can give parents more flexibility in how they share the care of their child in the first year following birth or adoption. Parents can share up to 50 weeks of leave and up to 37 weeks of pay and choose to take the leave and pay in a more flexible way (each parent can take up to 3 blocks of leave, more if their employer allows, interspersed with periods of work).

Eligible parents can be off work together for up to 6 months or alternatively stagger their leave and pay so that one of them is always at home with their baby in the first year.

Who can apply for Shared Parental Leave?

To trigger the right to SPL for one or both parents, the mother/adopter must:

- have a partner
- be entitled to:
- maternity/adoption leave
- to statutory maternity/adoption pay
- maternity allowance (if not eligible for maternity/adoption leave)
- have curtailed, or given notice to reduce, their maternity/adoption leave, pay or allowance.

A parent who intends to take SPL must:

- be an employee
- share the primary responsibility for the child with the other parent at the time of the birth or placement for adoption
- have properly notified their employer of their entitlement and have provided the necessary declarations and evidence.

In addition, a parent wanting to take SPL is required to satisfy the 'continuity of employment test' and their partner must meet the 'employment and earnings test'.

Continuity of Employment test	Employment and earnings test
The individual has worked for the same employer for at least 26 weeks at the end of the 15th week before the child's expected due date/matching and is still working for the	In the 66 weeks leading up to the baby's expected due

Continuity of Employment test	Employment and earnings test
employer at the start of each leave period.	date/matching date, the person has worked for at least 26 weeks and earned an average of at least £30 a week in any 13 weeks.

Sometimes only one parent will be eligible. For example a self-employed parent will not be entitled to SPL themselves but they may still pass the employment and earnings test so their partner, if they are an employee, may still qualify. If both parents are employees and meet the qualifying requirements then there will be a joint entitlement. The parents will have to decide how to divide the leave entitlement once the mother/adopter has decided to curtail their maternity/ adoption leave.

Shared Parental Pay

From April 2018, Statutory Shared Parental Pay is paid at £145.18 or 90% of an employee's average weekly earnings (whichever is lower). If the mother or adopter curtails their entitlement to maternity/adoption pay or maternity allowance before they have used their full entitlement then Statutory Shared Parental Pay can be claimed for any remaining weeks.

To qualify for Statutory Shared Parental Pay a parent must pass the continuity of employment test and have earned an average salary of the lower earnings limit of £116 for the 8 weeks' prior to the 15th week before the expected due date or matching date. The other parent in the family must meet the employment and earnings test.

How to apply for leave and pay

Having an early and informal discussion can provide an opportunity for both the employee and employer to talk about their preference regarding when Shared Parental Leave is taken.

It can also be an opportunity to discuss when any discontinuous leave can be best accommodated if appropriate. If an employee wishes to take Shared Parental Leave they must notify their employer of their entitlement **at least eight weeks before the start** of any Shared Parental Leave starts.

It is good practice for an employer to confirm they have received and accept this notification.

Each eligible parent can give their employer up to 3 separate notices booking or varying leave, although each must be given at least eight weeks before the leave is due to start. Each notice can be for a single block of leave, or the notice may be for a pattern of "discontinuous" leave involving different periods of leave. If a parent asks for a continuous block of leave the employer is required to agree to it. However, where the notification is for discontinuous blocks of leave the employer can refuse and require that the total weeks of leave in the notice be taken in a single continuous block. It is therefore beneficial for the employee and employer to discuss and attempt to agree a way in which the different blocks of leave can be taken.

Handling an application for SPL

Depending on the circumstances involved, there are four outcomes available to an employer once they have received, considered and discussed a Shared Parental Leave notification. It is important to note an employer **cannot refuse a notification for continuous leave**.

A) Confirm a continuous leave period or accept a discontinuous leave request.

B) Agree a modification to a leave request (an employee is under no obligation to modify a continuous leave notice and should never be put under any pressure to do so).

C) Refuse a discontinuous leave notification.

D) Whilst it is not good practice and should be avoided, it is possible for an employer to make no response to a leave notification.

For outcomes **C** and **D** above, the employee can withdraw their notification on or before the 15th calendar day after the notification was originally made and it will not count as one of their three notifications. If not, they must take the total amount of leave notified in one continuous block. The employee can choose when this leave period will begin within 19 days of the date the notification was given to the employer but it cannot start sooner than the initial notified start date. If they don't, the leave will begin on the starting date stated in the original notification.

Employers may wish to develop a policy that sets out the rules and procedures for applying for and taking Shared Parental Leave.

Some organisations offer enhanced maternity rights, giving mothers maternity pay above the statutory minimum, for example 26 weeks' full pay followed by 13 weeks SMP. Organisations may wish to "mirror" their maternity enhancements in any Shared Parental Leave policy.

There is no established statutory requirement to mirror occupational maternity schemes when a Shared Parental Leave scheme is established. The important thing is that within a Shared Parental Leave scheme, men and women are treated equally and paid at the same rate in the same circumstances.

New entitlement to Parental Bereavement Leave and Pay

The Government is introducing a new workplace right to Parental Bereavement Leave and Pay for parents who lose a child under the age of 18, including those who suffer a stillbirth from 24 weeks of pregnancy. The Parental Bereavement (Leave and Pay) Act gained Royal Assent in September 2018. Work is underway to get the Regulations ready to be laid before Parliament in 2019, with the intention that they will apply from the common commencement date of 6 April 2020.

Who will be entitled?

Employed parents who lose a child under the age of 18 (or those who suffer stillbirth from 24 weeks) will be entitled to 2 weeks of Parental Bereavement Leave as a 'day-one' right. Those with at least 26 weeks continuous service at the date of their child's death and earnings above the Lower Earnings Limit will also be entitled to Parental Bereavement Pay, paid at the statutory flat weekly rate of £145.18 (or 90% of average earnings, where this is lower).

The definition of a 'bereaved parent' is guided by the principle that those who are the 'primary carers' of the child should be the focus of the entitlement. The entitlement will apply to the child's 'legal' parents; individuals with a court order to give them day-to-day responsibility for caring for the child; and primary carers who do not have legal status, such as kinship carers. In all cases, eligibility will be based on facts that will be clear to both the employee and their employer in order to minimise confusion.

How can the leave and pay be taken?

Eligible parents will be able to take both the leave and pay as either a single block or one or two weeks, or as two separate blocks of one week of leave and/or pay (taken at different times). The employee will have 56 weeks from the date of their child's death in which to take the entitlement so as to allow parents to take the leave (and pay) at important moments, such as anniversaries, if they wish.

What notices will be required?

No prior notice will be required for leave taken very soon after the death. This will apply for a set number of weeks, in recognition that employees are likely to need to take leave at little or no notice. Employees will, however, be required to tell their employer that they are absent from work – informal notification will be acceptable. If leave is taken at a later point in time, a notice requirement will apply. The proposed notice period is at least one week.

Prior notice will be required for Parental Bereavement Pay irrespective of when the pay is taken. This is in order to give employers time to process the request.

What will the evidence requirements be?

The Government is considering whether employers should be able to request evidence of entitlement to Parental Bereavement Leave where an employee is required to give notice (i.e. where the leave is taken at a later date). Where they do, the Government proposes that this should be in the form of a written declaration that the employee meets eligibility criteria for leave (this is the approach used for Paternity Leave and Pay). This means that employers will not be able to ask parents for evidence of the child's death (e.g. they will not be able to ask for a copy of the death certificate) nor of their relationship with the child. However, when an employee needs to take time off work to grieve very soon after the death of their child, they will not be required to provide a written declaration before going on leave or subsequently. There will be no obligation on employers to ask for this information, and no obligation on employees to provide it (i.e. it will not be part of the eligibility requirements). For Parental Bereavement Pay, a written declaration will always be required from the employee in order to safeguard employers and the Exchequer from potential abuse, as is the case for other family related pay entitlements. The Parental Bereavement (Leave and Pay) Act 2018 applies only to Great Britain. At the current time, no legislation to introduce parental bereavement leave or pay has been introduced in Northern Ireland, therefore, the measure will not apply in Northern Ireland.

Adoption leave and pay

Qualifying employees who have been matched with a child may take up to 52 weeks adoption leave, and may be entitled to 39 weeks of statutory adoption pay. If a couple jointly adopt a child, one may take adoption leave and the other parent may be able to take paternity leave or shared parental leave.

Key points (overleaf)

The main adopter will be able to take paid time off for up to five adoption appointments. The secondary adopter will be entitled to take unpaid time off for up to two appointments. Adoption leave is a "day one" right there is no qualifying period.

Statutory Adoption Pay - the first six weeks will be paid at 90% of the employee's normal earnings. Some surrogate parents will become eligible for adoption leave. Adoption leave may be taken:

- When a child starts living with the employee or up to 14 days before the placement date (UK adoptions).
- When an employee has been matched with a child by a UK adoption agency.
- When the child arrives in the UK or within 28 days (overseas adoption).

The partner of an individual who adopts, or the secondary adopter if a couple are adopting jointly may be entitled to paternity leave and pay or shared parental leave. Employees must give their employer documentary proof to show that they have the right to paid Statutory Adoption Leave. This is usually a matching certificate from the adoption agency. The adoption agency must be recognised in the UK.

Statutory adoption leave can start either:

- from the date the child starts living with the employee

64

- up to 14 days before the date the child is expected to start living with the employee.

Employees should tell the employer within seven days of being told that they have been matched with a child, if this is not possible they must tell the employer as soon as possible. Employees who request or take adoption leave are protected against suffering a detriment or unfair dismissal. They have a right to return to the same job after 26 weeks adoption leave and after 52 weeks a suitable alternative job must be found.

Statutory Adoption Pay

Since April 2015, the rate of statutory adoption pay has been £139.58 per week. For the first six weeks the employee will be entitled to 90% of their normal earnings. The following 33 weeks will be paid at the statutory adoption pay rate. Some employers may offer to pay more than this - if they do it may form part of the terms and conditions of the employment contract. From 2 April 2017, the rate will be £140.98.

Keep in touch day

Both parties should agree when and how the employer will keep in contact, this may be via email, telephone contact etc. Employees should also agree with their employer if they will work the "keeping in touch" days, these can be used for training days, team events etc.
Up to ten keeping in touch days can be worked, and there is no provision for these days to be paid, this should be agreed between employee and employer. Statutory Adoption Pay may be paid or this may be off set against any contractual pay agreed.

Other benefits available if your child is disabled

Disability Living Allowance and Personal Independence Payment

If you have a disabled child under 16, you may be able to claim a benefit called Disability Living Allowance (DLA) for them. DLA has two components. The mobility component may be paid if your child has problems with getting around, and the care component may be paid if they have care needs which are more than most children of their age.

You cannot get the mobility component for a child under three. There is no age requirement for the care component, but you cannot usually claim it for a baby under three months old. This is because your child must have had care needs or mobility problems for at least three months before they can be entitled to DLA, unless they are terminally ill. It can be difficult to claim DLA for a young child and it may help to get specialist advice.

If your child is 16 or over and on DLA, they will be invited to claim Personal Independence Payment (PIP) instead of DLA, unless they are terminally ill (when they stay on DLA until their award expires). There is more information about the move to PIP on the Contact a Family website.

If your child is 16 or over and doesn't have an existing DLA claim, they will have to claim PIP.

DLA and PIP, claimed for you or your children, do not depend on income so are not affected when you move into or out of paid work.

DLA and PIP are complex benefits. It is advisable to seek personal advice when applying because the claim forms are long and you are more likely to be successful with professional advice.

DLA and PIP are 'passports' to other benefits and services – for example, you may get more Child Tax Credit (see below) if your child receives DLA or PIP.

Child Benefit and Child Tax Credit

You should also be able to claim Child Benefit and Child Tax Credit for your child. You may get more Child Tax Credit if your child gets DLA or PIP, because there is an extra element of Child Tax Credit included in the calculation. Make sure you tell the Tax Credit Office what rate of DLA or PIP your child is getting. In some areas of the country, if you are making a new claim for Child Tax Credit you will be told to claim Universal Credit instead. This also has extra elements for children on DLA or PIP.

Working Tax Credit (WTC)

WTC can be claimed by a lone working parent or a couple in which one or both partners work (see Working Tax Credit). The basic amount you are awarded is tapered off as your income increases. You may also qualify for help with childcare costs (see Childcare element of Working Tax Credit).

If your disabled child is 16 or over and works 16 hours or more, they may be able to claim WTC themselves, as long as they receive DLA or PIP (see Working Tax Credit). You should get advice if you need to make decisions about whether you claim for your child or they claim for themselves (see transition guide). You can't get Child Benefit or Child Tax Credit for a young person who claims WTC.

In some parts of the country, someone making a new claim for Working Tax Credit will be told to claim Universal Credit (UC) instead. You can't get Child Benefit or Child Tax Credit for a young person who claims UC. If you are not sure whether a young person does have to claim UC, get advice, as it can be less generous than Working Tax Credit.

Carer's Allowance

If you are a carer for your disabled child and they get the middle or higher rate care component of DLA, or the daily living component of PIP, you may be able to get Carer's Allowance. If you are thinking of taking up work you may want to consider the effect it may have on your entitlement to Carer's Allowance.

Employment and Support Allowance (ESA)

Over 16s who are not working and would have difficulty working because of illness or disability can claim Employment and Support Allowance (ESA) (see Benefits for disabled adults). The test for ESA can be quite difficult to meet and it is worth getting advice if your child is unsuccessful. Young people claiming DLA/PIP can claim ESA while still in education. However, you can't claim Child Benefit or Child Tax Credit at the same time as your young person claims ESA, so you may need advice about which to claim, or you can research the amounts involved. You can look at the different benefit amounts which would be paid depending on who claims by using an online calculator like the one on the website Turn2Us. Even if your young person claims ESA, you can still be their appointee for the benefit, if that is necessary (that means you would be responsible for making the claim and reporting all changes of circumstances).

In some parts of the country, a young person claiming income-related ESA will be told to claim Universal Credit (UC) instead. You can be an appointee for UC if necessary (it is usually claimed online). You can't claim Child Benefit or Child Tax Credit for a young person who is claiming UC, so you may need advice. UC can be less generous than income-related ESA, for example if your child gets PIP, and/or is thinking of working, so also get advice if you are not sure if they do have to claim UC.

Direct Payments (DP)

If your disabled child, having been assessed by your local authority, is entitled to services, you can choose to have direct payments (DP) and buy the services yourself. DP are for the stipulated services and are not affected by what you earn.

Disabled Facilities Grant

If your local authority provides a grant to alter your home to suit your disabled child's needs it is not affected by your income.

Housing Benefit and Council Tax Reduction

Housing Benefit and Council Tax Reduction (help with the council tax from your local authority) depend on your income. These benefits also depend on how many dependent children you have and the calculation will be different if your children are on DLA or PIP, so make sure the local authority know about this. In addition, the number of bedrooms allowed for in the Housing Benefit (HB) calculation could be higher if your children are unable to share a room because of disability and they are on DLA or PIP. Again make sure the local authority are aware.

In some areas of the country, if you make a new claim for Housing Benefit, you will be told to claim Universal Credit instead. The same bedroom rules apply.

If you move into work, you may, depending on your income, still be entitled to such help but you need to inform your local authority for the benefits to be recalculated. You can use the calculator at the website www.turn2us.org.uk to check your entitlement.

Family Fund

The Family Fund gives discretionary grants to families with severely disabled children under 18. They have their own definition of 'severely disabled'. The grants are for things not supplied by statutory authorities. Usually the grants are made to families on benefits, but the fund may also be able to help other families on low incomes.

Help with health costs

You can qualify for help with health costs, for example prescriptions and sight tests, if you receive some benefits such as Income Support, Income-based Jobseeker's Allowance, Income-related Employment and Support Allowance, or the Guarantee credit of Pension Credit . Some people on Universal Credit or tax credits may be entitled, and you may also be able to apply for help if you are on a low income. Prescriptions are free for under 16s, and under 19s in full-time education.

Fore a more detailed breakdown of welfare benefits and amounts please refer to appendix 1.

****

Useful contacts

Attendance Allowance helpline 0800 731 0122 Textphone 0800 731 0317

Carer's Allowance Unit 0800 731 0297 (textphone: 0800 731 0317)

DWP Bereavement Service:

Telephone: 0800 731 7469
Textphone: 0800 731 0464

Department for Work and pensions
www.gov.uk/government/organisations/department-for-work-pensions

Winter Fuel Payments Helpline 0800 731 0160

Disability benefits Advice
www.gov.uk/disability-benefits-helpline
0800 121 4433
Textphone 0800 121 4493

Jobcentre Plus 0800 055 6688 textphone 0800 023 4888

Pension Credit claim line 0800 99 1234 (textphone: 0800 169 0133).

Royal National Institute for the Blind 0303 123 9999
www.rnib.org.uk.

Tax Credit helpline 0345 300 3900 (textphone 0345 300 3909).

TV Licence concessions 0300 790 6165

Universal Credit helpline 0845 600 0723 (textphone 0845 600 0743).

Child benefit helpline 0300 200 3100: textphone 0300 200 3103

Family Fund 0844 974 4099 Online www.familyfund.org.uk

Healthy Start Helpline 0845 607 6823 www.healthystart.nhs.uk

www.nurserymilk.co.uk.

*****

Chapter 5

Disabled People and Education

Education and the law

It's against the law for a school or other education provider to treat disabled students unfavourably. This includes: 'direct discrimination', eg refusing admission to a student because of disability; 'indirect discrimination', eg only providing application forms in one format that may not be accessible; 'discrimination arising from a disability', eg a disabled pupil is prevented from going outside at break time because it takes too long to get there; 'harassment', eg a teacher shouts at a disabled student for not paying attention when the student's disability stops them from easily concentrating and victimisation, eg suspending a disabled student because they've complained about harassment.

Reasonable adjustments

As with employers, an education provider has a duty to make 'reasonable adjustments' to make sure disabled students are not discriminated against. These changes could include changes to physical features, eg creating a ramp so that students can enter a classroom,providing extra support and aids (like specialist teachers or equipment)

Portage

It is worth at this point mentioning portage, which can benefit your child pre-school. Portage is a home-visiting educational service for pre-school children with additional support needs and their families. Portage Home Visitors are employed by Local Authorities and Charities to support children and families within their local community. The Portage model of learning is characterised by the following attributes:

- regular home visiting;
- supporting the development of play, communication, relationships, and learning for young children within the family;
- supporting the child and family's participation and inclusion in the community in their own right;
- working together with parents within the family, with them taking the leading role in the partnership that is established;
- helping parents to identify what is important to them and their child and plan goals for learning and participation;
- keeping a shared record of the child's progress and other issues raised by the family;
- responding flexibly to the needs of the child and family when providing support;
- You can find out more about Portage by contacting The National Portage Association address at the end of the chapter.

Special Educational Needs (SEN)

All publicly-funded pre-schools, nurseries, state schools and local authorities must try to identify and help assess children with Special Educational Needs. If a child has a statement of special educational needs, they should have a 'transition plan' drawn up in Year 9. This helps to plan what support the child will have after leaving school.

Higher education

All universities and higher education colleges should have a person in charge of disability issues that you can talk to about the support they offer. You can also ask local social services for an assessment to help with your day-to-day living needs.

Special educational needs support

Your child will get SEN support at their school or college. Your child may need an education, health and care (EHC) plan if they need more support than their school provides.

Children under 5

SEN support for children under 5 includes:

- a written progress check when your child is 2 years old
- a child health visitor carrying out a health check for your child if they're aged 2 to 3
- a written assessment in the summer term of your child's first year of primary school
- making reasonable adjustments for disabled children, like providing aids like tactile signs

Nurseries, playgroups and childminders registered with Ofsted follow the Early Years Foundation Stage (EYFS) framework. The framework makes sure that there's support in place for children with SEND.

Talk to a doctor or health adviser if you think your child has SEND but they don't go to a nursery, playgroup or childminder. They'll tell you what support options are available.

Children between 5 and 15

Talk to the teacher or the SEN co-ordinator (SENCO) if you think your child needs:

- a special learning programme
- extra help from a teacher or assistant
- to work in a smaller group
- observation in class or at break
- help taking part in class activities
- extra encouragement in their learning, eg to ask questions or to try something they find difficult
- help communicating with other children
- support with physical or personal care difficulties, eg eating, getting around school safely or using the toilet

Young people aged 16 or over in further education

Contact the college before your child starts further education to make sure that they can meet your child's needs. The college and your local authority will talk to your child about the support they need.

Extra help

An education, health and care (EHC) plan is for children and young people aged up to 25 who need more support than is available through special educational needs support. EHC plans identify educational, health and social needs and set out the additional support to meet those needs.

Requesting an EHC assessment

You can ask your local authority to carry out an assessment if you think your child needs an EHC plan.

A young person can request an assessment themselves if they're aged 16 to 25.

A request can also be made by anyone else who thinks an assessment may be necessary, including doctors, health visitors, teachers, parents and family friends. If they decide to carry out an assessment you may be asked for:

- any reports from your child's school, nursery or childminder
- doctors' assessments of your child
- a letter from you about your child's needs

The local authority will tell you within 16 weeks whether an EHC plan is going to be made for your child.

Creating an EHC plan

Your local authority will create a draft EHC plan and send you a copy. You have 15 days to comment, including if you want to ask that your child goes to a specialist needs school or specialist college. Your local authority has 20 weeks from the date of the assessment to give you the final EHC plan.

Disagreeing with a decision

You can challenge your local authority about:

- their decision to not carry out an assessment
- their decision to not create an EHC plan
- the special educational support in the EHC plan
- the school named in the EHC plan

If you can't resolve the problem with your local authority, you can appeal to the Special Educational Needs and Disability (SEND) Tribunal.

Personal budgets

You may be able to get a personal budget for your child if they have an EHC plan or have been told that they need one. It allows you to have a say in how to spend the money on support for your child.

There are 3 ways you can use your personal budget. You can have:

- direct payments made into your account - you buy and manage services yourself
- an arrangement with your local authority or school where they hold the money for you but you still decide how to spend it (sometimes called 'notional arrangements')
- third-party arrangements - you choose someone else to manage the money for you

You can have a combination of all 3 options.

Independent support for children of all ages

Independent supporters can help you and your child through the new SEN assessment process, including:

- replacing a statement of special educational needs with a new EHC plan
- moving a child from a learning difficulty assessment (LDA) to an EHC plan

You can find out how to get local support through:

- Council for Disabled Children

- Information, Advice and Support Service Network
- your local authority website and search for 'Local Offer'

If your child got support before September 2014

Your child will continue to get support until they're moved across to special educational needs (SEN) support or an education, health and care (EHC) plan. Your child should have moved to:

- o SEN Support by summer 2015 if they already got help through School Action, School Action Plus, Early Years Action or Early Years Action Plus
- o an EHC plan by spring 2018 if they have a statement
- o an EHC plan by September 2016 if they have an LDA

Early Years Action and School Action

This support is either a different way of teaching certain things, or some help from an extra adult.

Early Years Action Plus and School Action Plus

This is extra help from an external specialist, eg a speech therapist.

Assessments

An assessment of special educational needs involves experts and people involved in your child's education. They ask about your child's needs and what should be done to meet them.

Statement

A statement of special education needs describes your child's needs and how they should be met, including what school they should go to.

Further education

If your child has a statement of special educational needs, they'll have a 'transition plan' drawn up in Year 9. This helps to plan for their future after leaving school.

Disabled people and financing studies

Financial support for all students comes in the form of tuition fee loans, means tested loans for living expenses and also a range of supplementary grants and loans depending on individual circumstances. Entitlement to student support depends on where you are living and where you intend to study. For details of loan entitlement and rates also Bursaries, you should contact:

Student finance England if you reside in England
www.gov.uk/student-finance

Northern Ireland Student finance NI 0300 100 0077
www.studentfinanceni.co.uk

Scotland Student Awards Agency for Scotland www.saas.gov.uk

Wales Student Finance Wales 0300 400 4050
www.studentfianncewales.co.uk

For details of loans and bursaries plus other sources of finance, you should contact the student support officer responsible for advice at the educational institution that you are to attend.

Students and means tested benefits

If you are a disabled student and want more information on benefits entitlement and how being a student in higher education affects benefits then you should contact the Disability Advisor at your local Jobcentre Plus. Essentially, benefit entitlement will depend very much on your individual circumstances and what type of education you are undertaking.

*****

Useful contacts

Contact a Family helpline
helpline@cafamily.org.uk
Telephone: 0808 808 3555

Independent Parental Special Education Advice (IPSEA).
24-26 Gold Street
Saffron Walden
Essex
CB10 1EJ
www.ipsea.org.uk
Telephone: 01799 582030 (Monday to Friday, 9am-5pm)

National Portage Association
Kings Court
17 School Road
Birmingham
B28 8JG Tel: 0121 244 1807
Fax: 0121 244 1801

www.portage.org.uk
General Enquiries info@portage.org.uk

***

Chapter 6

Help With Transport and Equipment for You and Your Disabled Child

---

You can obtain help and assistance with transport and equipment, which is designed specifically to make life easier for you and your child. Assistance with transport and equipment will also help to foster independence for your child.

This chapter outlines the main sources of transport and equipment available for you, but for more detailed advice about equipment for use inside and outside your home you should discuss this with your occupational therapist.

Welfare benefits

We covered welfare benefits in chapter 4. In addition to the various welfare benefits available to assist you with transport, there are other schemes, the most important being the schemes to help you buy a car and the Blue Badge Scheme that relates to parking for the disabled. You can also get exemption from Vehicle Road Tax.

The Blue Badge Scheme
Blue Badge parking concessions-What is the Blue Badge Scheme?

The aim of the Blue Badge scheme is to help disabled people who have severe mobility problems to access goods, services and other facilities by allowing them to park close to their destination. The scheme provides a national range of on-street parking concessions for Blue Badge holders who are travelling either as a driver or passenger.

People who automatically qualify for a badge

You're automatically eligible for a Blue Badge if you:

- are registered as blind
- get the higher rate of the mobility component of Disability Living Allowance (DLA)
- get Personal Independence Payment (PIP) and scored 8 points or more in the 'moving around' area of your assessment - check your decision letter if you're not sure
- get War Pensioners' Mobility Supplement
- received a lump sum payment as part of the Armed Forces Compensation scheme (tariffs 1 to 8), and have been certified as having a permanent and substantial disability

People who may also qualify for a badge

It's worth applying as you might still be able to get a badge. You'll have to fill in an extra part of the application to show why you need one.

You should do this if:

- you have problems walking that are permanent, or that your doctor says are likely to last at least a year
- you can't use your arms
- you're applying on behalf of a child aged over 2 who has problems walking, or a child under 3 who needs to be close to a vehicle because of a health condition

You can find out more about the Blue Badge Scheme and whether you are entitled by contacting your local council. Alternatively, you can contact the National blue badge helpline on 0800 0699 784.

The Motability Scheme

he Motability Scheme helps disabled people get mobile by exchanging their mobility allowance to lease a car, scooter or powered wheelchair. To be eligible to join the Scheme, you need to receive one of the following mobility allowances and must have at least 12 months' award length of your allowance remaining.

Higher Rate Mobility Component of Disability Living Allowance (HRMC DLA)

This allowance is provided by the Department for Work and Pensions (DWP) and can be used to cover the cost of a lease agreement with Motability Operations Ltd. As of 11 April 2018, this allowance is £59.75 per week.

As part of its welfare reform programme, the Government has started to replace Disability Living Allowance (DLA) with a new benefit called Personal Independence Payment (PIP) for disabled people aged between 16 and 64. The Motability Scheme works with PIP in the same way as is it does with DLA. For more information, go to dwp.gov.uk/pipOpens in new window . As of 09 April 2018, this allowance is £59.75 per week.

War Pensioners' Mobility Supplement (WPMS)

This allowance is provided by Veterans UKOpens in new window and can be used to cover the cost of a lease agreement with

Motability Operations Ltd. As of 11 April 2018, this allowance is £66.75 per week.

Armed Forces Independence Payment (AFIP)

A new allowance called Armed Forces Independence Payment (AFIP) was introduced as part of the Welfare Reform Act 2012. Those who receive this allowance will be eligible to join the Motability Scheme. For more information, visit Veterans UK websiteOpens in new window . As of 11 April 2018, this allowance is £59.75 per week (this refers to the mobility element, which is the same rate as HRMC DLA and ERMC PIP).

If you are visiting the Car Search or Scooter and Powered Wheelchair Search to compare and choose a Motability vehicle, please refer to the DLA/PIP option when making your allowance choice on the relevant option.

The Attendance Allowance cannot be used to lease a car through the Motability Scheme

You may not have to pay VAT on having a vehicle adapted to suit your condition, or on the lease of a Motability vehicle - this is known as VAT relief.

There are currently over 640,000 people enjoying the benefits of Motability. The following are included in the package:

- A brand new car, powered wheelchair or scooter every three years, or Wheelchair Accessible Vehicle (WAV) every five years
- Insurance, servicing and maintenance
- Full breakdown assistance

- Annual vehicle tax
- Replacement tyres (and batteries for scooters and wheelchairs)

- Windscreen repair or replacement
- 60,000 mileage allowance over three years for cars; 100,000 for WAVs
- Many adaptations at no extra cost
- Two named drivers for your car

The Motability Scheme is directed and overseen by Motability, a national charity that also raises funds and provides financial assistance to customers who would otherwise be unable to afford the mobility solution they need.

Motability Operations is a company responsible for the finance, administration and maintenance of Motability cars, scooters and powered wheelchairs.

To find out more about Motability you should contact them at the address at the end of this chapter.

Use of Public Transport

Travel permits for buses and trains

Most local authorities offer travel permits for children who are disabled and over the age of 5 years. There is normally a charge, as there is with everything and the criteria and availability of the permists will vary according to each authority, generally however, the main criteria is being in receipt of the higher rate of PIP. In some cases, your child's GP may be asked for a supporting letter. Your local council will be able to help in this regard.

Help with taxi fares

Some local councils, but not all, offer help with the cost of Black Cab taxi fares. The criteria is similar to other concessions. You should ask at your local council for details.

Community transport schemes

Many local authorities offer local community transport schemes for people with mobility problems. Again, the local authority will have details of schemes on offer in your area. There is also a national association, the Community Transport Association. The CTA is a national membership association which leads and supports community transport. Address at the end of this chapter.

Equipment available for disabled children-Equipment provision through local authorities & direct payments

Much of the equipment need by you or your child, may be provided by your local authority. This will usually occur following an assessment and recommendation by an occupational therapist and will depend on the eligibility criteria of your local authority. If your child is eligible, the equipment will be provided on a long-term loan basis. This means that the equipment will remain the property of the council, but that your child can use it for as long as they need it. The council will take responsibility for the servicing and maintenance of the equipment.

Direct payments

If your child's occupational therapy assessment shows that they need a piece of equipment but you prefer an alternative piece of equipment that meets the same need, you may be able to have a direct payment. It is now mandatory for local authorities to offer the choice of direct payments.

A direct payment is a cash payment that equals the amount it costs your local authority to supply their choice of standard equipment. You can then add your own money to this ('top-up') to buy your preferred piece of equipment. For example, your local authority may provide you with a bath lift that has a fixed angle backrest and you may wish to pay for a bath lift that has a reclining backrest. Usually you will be the joint owner of the equipment with your local authority.

Before you purchase the equipment, your local authority must be satisfied that your child's needs will be met by the item you have chosen, and that the equipment is safe. You will also need to agree with your local authority who will be responsible for the servicing and maintenance of the equipment. Following purchase, you will need to provide proof of purchase and your local authority will review the equipment to ensure safety and suitability. Note that if you receive direct payments to arrange your child's care and support at home then this must not be used to buy equipment.

Arranging an assessment

To enquire about an assessment with an occupational therapist contact your local social services. You can obtain their contact details by entering your postcode on the directgov website.

Wheelchairs

If you have a long-term or permanent difficulty with mobility, getting a wheelchair or scooter, or other mobility equipment, may help you to live more independently.

Again, you will need to consult an occupational therapist who will provide you with the advice appropriate to your specific situation. there are wheelchairs centres in each local authority area and in Scotland and Wales they are called Aritificial limb and appliance centres and in Northern Ireland they are called Prosthetic and Orthotic Aids Centres.

Other needs such as nappies and incontinence pads

If you require nappies or incontince pads, and your child is over the age of infancy, as a result of an ongoing disability, you should contact your local health authority. Your GP can advise you about what is avialble or at least point you in the right direction, as can the Health Visitor or Community Paediatrician.

Adaptations to your housing-Disabled Facilities Grants

You could get a grant from your council if your child is disabled and you need to make changes to your home, for example to widen doors and install ramps, improve access to rooms and facilities - eg stairlifts or a downstairs bathroom, provide a heating system suitable for your needs, adapt heating or lighting controls to make them easier to use.

A Disabled Facilities Grant will not affect any benefits that you're getting. How much you get depends on your household income and household savings over £6,000

Country	Grant
England	Up to £30,000
Wales	Up to £36,000
Northern Ireland	Up to £25,000
Scotland	Disabled Facilities Grants are not available - find out about support for equipment and adaptations

Depending on your income, you may need to pay towards the cost of the work to the property. Disabled children under 18 can get a grant without their parents' income being taken into account. Contact your local council for more information. You might not get any grant if you start work on your property before the council approves your application.

How and when you will be paid

You'll be paid either by instalments - as the work progresses or in full - when the work is finished. The council may pay the contractor directly, or give you a cheque to pass on - they'll agree this with you when they approve your application. You'll be paid either when the council is happy with the finished work, when you give the council the invoice, demand or receipt for payment from the contractor. Normally, if you (or a relative) does the work the council will only accept invoices for materials or services you've bought.

Eligibility

You or someone living in your property must be disabled. Either you or the person you're applying for must:

- o   own the property or be a tenant
- o   intend to live in the property during the grant period (which is currently 5 years)
- o   You can also apply for a grant if you're a landlord and have a disabled tenant.

The council will needsto be happy that the work is necessary and appropriate to meet the disabled person's needs, reasonable and can be done - depending on the age and condition of the property. You might not get any grant if you start work on your property before the council approves your application.

****

Useful Contacts

Motability

www.motability.co.uk

Tel: 0300 456 4566 8am-7pm Monday to Friday 9am-1pm Saturday.

Blue badge Scheme

www.gov.uk/blue-badge-scheme-information-council

National blue badge helpline 0800 0699 784.

Community Transport Association

0345 1306195,

www.ctauk.org

Housing Ombudsman

info@housing-ombudsman.org.uk

Telephone: 0300 111 3000

Shelter England

www.shelter.org.uk

Help line 0808 800 4444

Disability Housing Scotland

www.housingoptionsscotland.org.uk

Independent Living For Disabled people

www.scope.org.uk

0808 800 3333

www.gov.uk/help-for-disabled-child

Deals with UK housing advice for disabled

Chapter 7

Holidays and Breaks for Disabled Children and Their Families

Everyone, whatever their situation, needs a break from their children every now and again. Having a breathing space from caring for a disabled child is no exception. Also, your disabled child is likely to enjoy the opportunity of doing new things with other children and adults and will also probably learn much from the experience.

In addition to breaks away from your child(ren) breaks away with your child are also important and there are many organisations which can help you plan a holiday with your disabled child.

In this chapter we outline some of the possibilities for short-term breaks or respite care, such as family based schemes, play schemes or residential care, and holidays. There is also a list of organisations which may be of use to you.

Respite breaks or short term breaks

Respite care is often used to describe the situation when a child goes away from the family home overnight to give his or her parent/carer a break. In addition, respite care can also apply to care given to a child in his or her own home whilst the parent/carer goes out, and to short-term breaks during the day, such as play schemes.

Many parents find it very hard to be away from their child, even when they really need the break. This is understandable but can be overcome by planning respite care so that you and your child can get to know someone over a space of time before you leave them in charge of your child. Because respite care may be needed in an emergency - if you were taken ill, for example, and there was no one else to care for your child - is it important for you to check out the respite care possibilities at an early stage before any crisis may occur.

Different types of respite care and short-term breaks are listed and described below.

Family Based Respite Care

Family based respite care schemes are usually run by local voluntary agencies or by social services departments. They assess, recruit, train and monitor single people or families who are able to look after a disabled child in their home on a regular basis, like 1 night a fortnight, a weekend per month, or sometimes longer spells like a week or a fortnight on occasions (e.g. once/twice a year) so the parent(s) can go away.

The procedure for recruiting, assessing and approving carers is very thorough and governed by Children Act 1989 guidelines (as amended by ongoing regulations) and is very similar to the procedure for recruiting foster parents. So you can rest assured from the start that the carer matched to your child is as suitable and capable as possible.

The scheme which recruits carers for a disabled child will have information about you and your child, what the child is like, what his or her disabilities are and what his or her likes and dislikes are. They will then match you and your child with a carer they judge to be suitable for your child. They will try and match racial, cultural and religious backgrounds as far as possible. It is then usual for you and your child to meet with the prospective carer and his or her own family on several occasions, at your home and the carer's home, to get to know each other. Only after a few meetings will it be possible for your child to stay overnight at the carer's home.

Family based respite care does not always have to mean overnight care though. Many carers are willing and able to take care of children during the day during the week on occasions (during the school holidays occasionally, for example) or sometimes at the weekend. This can normally be negotiated with the carer and who ever is running the scheme.

Residential Respite Care

Residential respite care units for disabled children are run by health, social services or voluntary agencies. They offer overnight care for your child on an emergency or regular basis, if you meet certain criteria which varies depending on the unit. If you are able to plan your child's first stay, it is always best to visit the unit with your child to meet the staff and look around the facilities. This will mean that parting from your child and seeing your child go away from home will be much easier for you both. You can find out about what residential respite care is available by asking your health professional, social services department or voluntary agency.

Play schemes and After School Clubs

Plays schemes for the school holidays and after school clubs are normally run by the leisure department of your local council, although some are also run by voluntary agencies. They are normally based in schools and offer play activities and outings in a relaxed but supervised environment.

Your child may be able to join the play schemes and clubs run for non-disabled children, depending on what his or her needs are. Special schemes and clubs are also run for disabled children.

Respite Care or Short-term Breaks in Your Home

There may be opportunities for respite care in your home meaning that your child can stay at home whilst you go out. This type of respite care, however, is not normally for overnights. Such breaks will usually be for care during the day, such as 2-4 hours, to give you time to go shopping, see some friends, or simply spend some time alone or with your partner. One of the main national organisations offering this type of care is the Carers Trust, which was a merger between Crossroads Caring For Carers Scheme and the Princess Royal Trust for Carers. They employ carers who go into families once a week for 4 hours or twice a week for 2 hours. Most families receive a maximum of 4 hours per week but this depends on their needs and circumstances. Carers work all hours so it is possible to have help at weekends and evenings as well as during the day. Carers Trust carers work with children and people of all ages and all disabilities.

Some local Crossroads Caring for Carers schemes also offer an occasional night sitting service if your sleep is often interrupted.

Some areas may not have a Carers Trust scheme but will have a similar scheme which works under a different name. Ask the Carers Trust national organisation (address at the end of this chapter) or your local social services department, health professional or voluntary organisation to see if you have a local scheme.

Holidays

Having a disabled child should not mean that you cannot go away. There are many organisations that can help you plan a holiday with your child or who can organise an independent trip for him or her if s/he is old enough.

The numerous organisations listed overleaf publish information

97

about holidays for the disabled including family holidays, activity holidays and holidays for unaccompanied disabled children and adults.

*****

Holiday Care

0843 289 2459

www.holiday-care.co.uk

Disability Rights UK

Plexal

14 East Bay Lane

Here East

Queen Elizabeth Olympic Park

Stratford

London

E20 3BS

Office Number: 0330 995 0400

This line is not an advice line. There are various different advice lines on the website.

Email: enquiries@disabilityrightsuk.o

Disability Holidays

Registered Office:

Unit 8 Victoria Way

Newmarket

Suffolk

CB8 7SH

Email: admin@disabilityholidaysguide.com

The following organisations can provide holidays and holiday accommodation for disabled children and their families.

Break

1 Montague Road
Schofield House,
Spar Road,
Norwich,
Norfolk NR6 6BX
Tel 01603 670100
email reception@break-charity.or
www.break-charity.org

Specialises in holidays for multiply disabled children and adults, individuals, groups and those unaccompanied by parents or staff

St Mark's Community Centre

218 Tollgate Road
Beckton
London
E6 5YA

Telephone: 01499 302715
Fax: 0207 473 7847
e-mail enquiries: contactus@across.org.uk

Organises holidays for disabled people of all ages across Europe

THE CALVERT TRUST

For all enquries relating to The Lake District Calvert Trust or general Calvert Trust questions please contact them using the details below.

Telephone: 017687 72255
Facsimile: 017687 71920
http://www.calvert-trust.org.uk/contact-us/lake-district

KESWICK

Little Crosthwaite
Keswick
Cumbria CA12 4QD
017687 72255
www.calvert-trust.keswick

EXMOOR

Wislandpound Farm
Kentisbury
North Devon EX31 4SJ
01598 763221
www.calvert-trust.org.uk/exmoor
The Calvert Trust in Northumberland, Cumbria and Devon have purpose built centres for disabled people and their families offering a wide range of sports and recreational activities.

3H Fund (Help the Handicapped Holiday Fund)
B2, Speldhurst Business Park,
Langton Road,
Speldhurst, Tunbridge Wells, Kent TN3 0AQ
Tel: 01892 860207
Email: info@3hfund.org.uk

Group holidays for physically disabled children and young people over 11 years.

FINANCING HOLIDAYS

Social Services/children's services

Disabled children and their families may be able to obtain a small grant from their social services department towards a holiday. The criteria for receiving some funding will vary from one council to another, but many means test and/or will only give money to a family every few years.

Charitable Organisations

MENCAP

The Membership Office
Mencap National Centre
123 Golden Lane
London EC1Y ORT
020 7454 0454
Email: holidayfund@mencap.org.uk

Provides grants towards the cost of a holiday for individuals with learning disabilities.

THE FAMILY FUND

Unit 4, Alpha Court
Monks Cross Drive
Huntington
York Y32 9WN
01904 550055
www.familyfund.org.uk
info@familyfund.org.uk

To receive funding, there must be a severely disabled child under the age of 16 in the family. Grants vary in size and can be used towards family holidays with or without the disabled child.

THE FAMILY HOLIDAY ASSOCIATION

3 Gainsford Street
London
SE1 2NE
020 3117 0650
www.familyholidayassociation.org.uk

The Family Holiday Association provides grants for families for one week's holiday of their choice. The family must be referred to the Association by social services, health professional or local voluntary organization. The child must be at least 3 years old.

PEARSON'S HOLIDAY FUND

P.O. Box 3017
South Croydon
CR2 9PN
02086 573053
www.pearsonsholidayfund.org.uk

Funds children aged 4-17 whilst on holiday in the U.K. The fund only deals with the referrer, i.e. the doctor, social worker, health visitor etc, rather than the family.

FAMILY ACTION

24 Angel Gate
City Road

London, EC1V 2PT

Tel: 020 7254 6251

www.fwa.org.uk

Provides grants for holidays to families with disabled children. Applications are made through social services or health professional.

Trains

Complaints and information-National Rail Enquiries Tel – 0845 748 4950. If you aren't happy with the way a train company deals with your complaint you can appeal, outside London, to: Passenger Focus (tel: 0300 123 2350).

In London-London Travel Watch at: http://www.londontravelwatch.org.uk/ (tel: 020 3176 2999).

Air Travel

Complaints and information- Civil Aviation Authority (CAA) at the address below:

Passenger Advice and Complaints Team

4th Floor,

CAA House

45-59 Kingsway

London

WC2B 6TE

Taxi and Mini cabs

Public Carriage Office (PCO) www.pco-licence.co.uk

Specialist companies

Access Travel

www.access-travel.co.uk

Tel: 07973 114365

Responsible Travel

Access Travel

Tel: 01273 823 700

www.responsibletravel.com

Enable Holidays

www.enableholidays.com

0871 222 4939

****

Chapter 8

Disability and Employment

Although this book is about the rights of disabled children, there might come a time, depending on the nature of your child's disability, when he or she wants to enter the workplace. This chapter covers the support and training available to help disabled people into work. It also covers employers responsibilities towards disabled people in the workplace.

Entering employment

The role of Jobcentre plus and Disability Employment Advisors

Jobcentre plus is the Department of Work and Pensions organisation providing benefits and services to people of working age. This means age 16 or over. Everyone who claims benefits from Jobcentre Plus is allocated a personal advisor to deal with claims for benefit and help them back into work. Disabled people also have access to a Disability Employment Advisor who provide employment assessment, job seeking advice and assistance with training as well as specialist advice and information. It is important to note that advice and support from a DEA is not dependant on benefits it is available to any disabled person.

Work programmes

There are a number of work programmes managed by 'providers' who are contracted by the government which aim to help people find work and stay in work. They provide activities such as work

106

experience, work trials, help to become self-employed, voluntary work, training and ongoing support. The programmes are mandatory if a person is considered capable of work. Referral to work programmes is normally through Jobcentre Plus. If in receipt of Job Seekers Allowance a person will have to take part in the Work Programme after nine months. If the advisor agrees a person may join earlier than this if they wish. If they receive Employment and Support Allowance the time for entry to a Work Programme will vary depending on an assessment of a person's fitness to work.

Community Work Placement Programme

The Community Work Placement Programme was designed for Jobseeker's Allowance claimants who require further support to obtain and sustain employment following a Work Programme placement. Participants had to undertake work placements for the benefit of the community and work-related activity. This programme was mandatory. It has now been withdrawn.

Work Choice

The work choice programme, which is now closed to new applicants, was aimed at people who were experiencing barriers to work arising from a disability or who were in work but risk losing their job as a result of a disability. Participation is voluntary and usually they must be referred by a Disability Employment Advisor. Work choice consists of two modules, each of which is tailored to their specific needs:

o Work Entry Support-this is up to six months help with vocational guidance, confidence building, job search advice and other support such as job application skills. In some cases, this support can be for longer than six months;

o In-Work Support-this is up to 12 months support once a person is in employment. The Work Choice Provider will work with them and their employer to identify the support needed and also help them develop the necessary skills and knowledge to move to unsupported employment;

Work choice was available throughout the UK with the exception of Northern Ireland where there are similar schemes.

Access to Work www.gov.uk/access-to-work

Access to Work is designed to help disabled people overcome any barriers that they may face in obtaining employment and retaining employment. Access to Work provides practical advice and also grants towards extra costs which may be incurred arising from a disability. This advice and support can include special aids and adaptations, or equipment needed for employment, adaptations premises (not new) and equipment, help with travel, help with a support worker, a communicator and, if needed, an interpreter.

Certain types of expenditure are excluded, details of which can be obtained during the application stage. Costs which are the responsibility of the employer, for example costs which are seen as a 'reasonable adjustment' under the Equality Act 2010, are not included. (See below for details of 'reasonable adjustments').

A person will be eligible for help through the Access to Work scheme if they are employed, including as an apprentice, self-employed or unemployed and have a job to start and they are disabled. Access to Work defines disability as in the Equality Act 2010 (see introduction) but also includes impairments and health conditions that are only evident in the workplace.

Access to Work also provides help to people with mental health conditions and learning difficulties. The service provides a wide range of support for a period of six months for people with mental health conditions, including work focussed mental health support tailored to the individual, assessment of an individuals needs, a personalised support plan, advice and guidance to employers and the identification of reasonable adjustments needed in the workplace.

How much support can a person receive?

If a person has been in a job for less than six weeks, are self-employed or are about to start work, Access to Work will cover 100% of approved costs. If they have been employed for six weeks or more when they apply for help, Access to Work will pay only some of the costs of support, called 'cost sharing' which is dependant on the number of employees in an organisation. The funding agreements can last up to three years with an annual review.

You can apply for access to work online or by phone, 0800 121 7459. Normally there will be a telephone interview by an advisor to assess eligibility.

Training

There are numerous government training programmes designed to help prepare people for work. Details can be found from a nearest Jobcentre Plus office. There are many courses available designed to help disabled people. Contact a disabled employment advisor at the local Jobcentre Plus office or ring the National Careers Service Helpline 0800 100 900 or Skills Development Scotland 0800 917 8000.

Benefits while training

DLA and PIP are not usually affected if training is undertaken or if a person gets a training allowance. However, DLA care component and PIP daily living component will not usually be paid for any days that a person stays in a care home to attend a residential training programme. The residential training programmes aim to help long-term unemployed adults overcome disability related barriers to employment.

Advice concerning benefits entitlement, such as Universal Credit Income Support, Jobseeker's allowance and Employment and Support Allowance and how they are affected by training, can be obtained from a local Jobcentre Plus.

When a person is in work

Disability and employers responsibilities

It's against the law for employers to discriminate against anyone because of a disability. The Equality Act 2010 protects everyone and covers areas including:

o   application forms

o   interview arrangements

o   aptitude or proficiency tests

o   job offers

o   terms of employment, including pay

o   promotion, transfer and training opportunities

o   dismissal or redundancy

o   discipline and grievances

Reasonable adjustments in the workplace

Those employees with disabilities share the same employment rights as other workers with the addition of some other rights as stated within the Equality Act 2010. Within this act, employers are expected to make 'reasonable adjustments' within the workplace with regard to access and facilities for disabled members of staff. The provisions set out in the Equality Act apply to every employer, no matter the size or industry (except the armed forces). It is worth noting that the reasonable adjustment requirements are not necessary to carry out in anticipation or only in case an employer gains a disabled employee. The adjustments need only be carried out once a disabled person is employed or applies for a role within the company.

To comply with the Equality Act 2010, an employee must suffer from severe or long-term impairments. Impairments of disabled employees include:

o Physical impairments - mobility disabilities

o Mental impairments - long term (12 months plus) mental illnesses or learning disabilities

o Sensory impairments - visual or hearing impairments.

What are reasonable adjustments?

The Equality Act states employers have a duty to amend the workplace in order to accommodate both disabled employees and/or applicants for job roles. These adjustments are in order to avoid disabled people being at a disadvantage when applying for a job or indeed working within an organisation. Reasonable adjustments can vary and cover areas from working arrangements to physical changes around the workplace.

Adjusted working arrangements may be flexible working hours to allow disabled employees to be able to meet their employment requirements, or amendments being made to workplace equipment, adapting it to suit employee's capabilities.

If a physical feature within the workplace creates a disadvantage for a disabled employee, steps must be taken to amend or remove the obstruction. Physical adjustments can include changes such as:

o The addition of a ramp rather than steps to access buildings.

o Providing disabled toilet facilities need to provided to accommodate those that need them.

o The widening of doorways to allow for wheelchair access.

o Repositioning door handles and/or light switches etc to ensure they can be reached.

In some cases, an employer may need to provide disabled employees with extra help through an aid to ensure that the disabled employee is not at any disadvantage against other workers. This aid may be in form of specialist or adapted equipment, such as special computer keyboards or telephones.

With regard to a disabled person applying for a job, an employer does not necessarily need to make the physical adjustments before the interview. It will suffice that an easily accessible location and necessary support and assistance for the applicant to get there is provided. If the applicant is then employed, the employer must consider the other adjustments mentioned above.

Recruitment

An employer who is recruiting staff may make limited enquiries about a person's health or disability. They can only be asked about their health or disability:

o to help decide if they can carry out a task that is an essential part of the work

o to help find out if they can take part in an interview

112

o to help decide if the interviewers need to make reasonable adjustments for them in a selection process

o to help monitoring

o if they want to increase the number of disabled people they employ

o if they need to know for the purposes of national security checks

A person may be asked whether they have a health condition or disability on an application form or in an interview. Thought needs to be given as to whether the question is one that is allowed to be asked at that stage of recruitment.

Redundancy and retirement

A person can't be chosen for redundancy just because they are disabled. The selection process for redundancy must be fair and balanced for all employees. Also, an employer cannot force a person to retire if they become disabled.

****

Useful Contacts

Access to Work.0800 121 7459

www.evenbreak.co.uk

Jobs for disabled people - Evenbreak matches disabled job seekers with employers looking to build a diverse workforce

Evenbreak

402 Metro Central Heights

London SE1 6DX

www.evenbreak.co.uk

Email Address:

info@evenbreak.co.uk

0845 658 5717

www.gov.uk/rights-disabled-person/employment

Industrial Injuries

www.jobcentrenearme.com/industrial-injuries-disablement-benefit/

0345 604 3719

National Careers Service Helpline 0800 100 900 or Skills Development Scotland 0800 917 8000.

*****

Adaptations, 7, 91
After School Clubs, 7, 96
Armed Forces, 161
Asthma, 20
Attendance Allowance, 119, 120, 121, 123, 124
Autistic spectrum disorders, 20

Bereavement Allowance, 119
Blue Badge parking, 84
Blue badge Scheme, 93

Care homes, 154
Carers Allowance, 119
Chronic fatigue syndrome, 20
Chronic fatigue syndrome (CFS),, 20
Clinical psychologist, 3, 31
Cold weather Payment, 119
Communication support worker, 3, 31
Community Transport Association, 89, 93
Community transport schemes, 89
Community Work Placement Programme, 107
Consumer law, 18
Council Tax Support, 119, 124

Dementia, 20
Department of Work and Pensions, 106
Depression, 11, 20
Disability Employment Advisors, 7, 106
Disability Living Allowance, 121, 123
Disabled children, 3, 27, 91
Disabled Facilities Grant, 91
Disfigurements, 22

Dyslexia, 20
Dyspraxia, 20

Early Years Action, 80
Education, 6, 74, 83
Educational psychologist, 3, 32
Employment and Support Allowance, 107, 110, 119, 135, 136, 161
Employment law, 18
Epilepsy, 20
Equality Act 2010, 3, 18, 43, 108, 110, 111

Family Based Respite Care, 7, 95
Family Fund, 73
Family law, 18
Fibromyalgia, 20

General practitioner (GP), 3, 32

Health visitor, 3, 32
Heart disease, 20
Higher education, 6, 76
HIV, 3, 21
Holidays, 7, 10, 94, 97, 99, 105
Housing Benefit, 119, 120, 123, 124, 125, 126, 129, 136, 161

Impairment, 19
Income Support, 110, 119, 128, 129, 130, 161

Job Seekers Allowance, 107, 119
Jobcentre plus, 7, 106

Key worker, 4, 32

Learning disabilities, 20
Learning disability nurses, 4, 33
Learning support assistant, 4, 33

Mental illnesses, 21
Motability, 6, 86, 87, 88, 93
Motability Scheme, 6, 86, 88
Motor neurone disease, 20
Multiple sclerosis, 21
Muscular dystrophy, 20
Myalgic encephalitis, 20

Named officer, 4, 33
Northern Ireland Student finance, 81

Paediatric neurologist, 4, 34
Paediatric occupational therapist, 4, 34
Paediatrician (Health Service), 4, 34
Pension Credit, 72, 119, 120, 123, 124, 125, 126, 127, 128, 152, 153, 161
Personal Independence Payment, 119, 120, 121, 123, 124
Physiotherapist, 4, 34
Play schemes, 7, 96
Portage, 4, 6, 34, 74, 75, 83
Portage home visitor, 4, 34, 75

Reasonable adjustments, 6, 8, 74, 110, 111
Recruitment, 112
Redundancy, 8, 113
Residential Respite Care, 7, 96
Respiratory conditions, 20

Respite breaks, 7, 94
Rheumatoid arthritis, 20

Schizophrenia, 21
School nurse, 4, 35
Short-term Breaks, 7, 97
Siblings, 3, 11, 14
Social worker (Childrens), 4, 35
Special Educational Needs (SEN, 6, 28, 75
Special educational needs co-ordinator (SENCO), 4, 35
Specialised activities, 3, 26
Stroke, 20
Student Awards Agency for Scotland, 81
Student finance England, 81
Student Finance Wales, 81
Systemic lupus erythematosis, 20

Tax Credits, 119
The Blue Badge Scheme, 6, 84
Thrombosis, 20
TV Licence Concessions, 119

Universal Credit, 73, 119, 123, 125, 135, 161

Welfare benefits, 6, 84, 119
Wheelchairs, 7, 90
Winter Fuel payment, 119
Work Choice, 107, 108
Work programmes, 106

****

Appendix 1

Welfare benefits generally-2018-2019

As pointed out in this book, only certain benefits may be relevant to a parent of a disabled child. These have been outlined in chapter 3. However, as a reference point the following overview of all benefits available to people, whether parents of a disabled child or not, should prove useful. The following benefits are outlined:

➢ Attendance Allowance
➢ Personal Independence Payment
➢ Carers Allowance
➢ Housing Benefit
➢ Council Tax Support
➢ Pension Credit
➢ Income Support
➢ Job Seekers Allowance
➢ Employment and Support Allowance
➢ Universal Credit
➢ Tax Credits
➢ Winter Fuel payment
➢ Cold weather Payment
➢ TV Licence Concessions
➢ Bereavement Allowance

Attendance Allowance

You should be able to claim Attendance Allowance if your ability to look after your own personal care is affected by physical or mental illness or disability. Attendance Allowance has 2 weekly rates, and

119

the rate you get very much depends on the help you need. The current rates are:

- £57.30 if you need help in the day or at night
- £85.60 if you need help both in the day and at night.

Claiming Attendance Allowance won't affect any other income you receive, and it's also tax-free. If you are awarded it, you may become entitled to other benefits, such as Pension Credit, Housing Benefit or Council Tax Reduction, or an increase in these benefits.

You may be eligible for Attendance Allowance if you are 65 or over (if you're under 65, you may be eligible for Personal Independence Payment instead-see below), could benefit from help with personal care, such as getting washed or dressed, or supervision to keep you safe during the day or night, have any type of disability or illness, including sight or hearing impairments, or mental health issues such as dementia and have needed help for at least 6 months. (If you're terminally ill you can make a claim straight away.)

Attendance Allowance isn't means-tested, so your income and savings aren't taken into account. You don't actually have to receive help from a carer, as Attendance Allowance is based on the help you need, not the help you actually get. Also, you don't strictly have to spend your Attendance Allowance on care – it's up to you how you use it. You can get a claim form by calling the Attendance Allowance helpline on 0800 731 0122.You can also download a claim form or claim online.

Attendance Allowance doesn't usually take into account problems with housework, cooking, shopping and gardening. If your application is turned down, ask an advice agency such as Citizens Advice about whether you should challenge the decision.

Many applications are turned down because people don't mention or aren't clear about how their illness or disability affects their lives.

Personal Independence Payment

Personal Independence Payment (PIP) is a benefit for people of working age with disabilities. It has replaced Disability Living Allowance (DLA) for anyone making a new claim. If you're under 65 and already claiming DLA you'll eventually be asked to claim PIP instead. If you were 65 or over on 8 April 2013 and already claiming DLA, you won't be affected by the change and you'll continue to get DLA payments for as long as you're entitled to them.

You may be eligible for PIP if you're under 65 and need help with daily living activities or help getting around, or both. If you are 65 or over and you have care needs, you can't claim PIP but you may be able to claim Attendance Allowance. If you are awarded PIP before you are 65 it can continue after age 65. PIP isn't based on National Insurance contributions and isn't means-tested. You can claim it whether you're working or not.

Rates of Personal Independence Payment

PIP has two parts – a **daily living component** and a **mobility component.** They're paid at different rates, depending on the level of difficulty you have performing particular activities such as preparing food and drink or dressing and undressing. You may be able to claim one or both components.

Daily living component:

Standard rate - £57.30week

Enhanced rate - £85.60 week

Mobility component:

Standard rate - £22.65 week
Enhanced rate - £59.75 week

To start your claim you'll need to call the Department for Work and Pensions (DWP) on 0800 917 2222 (textphone 0800 917 777). They will ask you for basic information and then send you a claim form. Most people will have to attend a face-to-face assessment of their needs as well. Find out more on the Gov.UK website. If your application is turned down contact an advice agency such as Citizens Advice about whether you should challenge the decision. Your needs may change and increase, so even if you're not eligible for PIP now, you may be able to claim successfully in the future.

Carer's Allowance – www.gov.uk/carers-allowance

The main welfare benefit for carers is called Carer's Allowance and it's worth £64.60 week if you're eligible. You don't have to be related to or live with the person you care for to claim Carer's Allowance. You'll also get National Insurance credits each week towards your pension if you're under pension age.

You may not think of yourself as a carer. Perhaps you've looked after someone for a long time without ever calling yourself one, or maybe you think the help you give your spouse or parent is simply what you should be doing. If so, you may have been missing out on the help that is available to you.

To claim Carer's Allowance, you must:

- spend at least 35 hours a week caring for a disabled person - you don't have to live with them
- care for someone who receives the higher- or middle-rate care component of Disability Living Allowance, either rate of Personal Independence Payment daily living component, or any rate of Attendance Allowance
- not earn more than £102 a week (after deductions)
- not be in full-time education.

Carer's Allowance may not be paid if you're receiving a State Pension or certain other benefits, but it's still worth claiming because you could get extra Pension Credit and/or Housing Benefit.

If you're claiming Universal Credit You may be able to get an extra amount because of your caring role without having to apply for Carer's Allowance. (see below for universal credit).

If you want to make a claim for carers allowance call the Carer's Allowance Unit on 0800 731 0297 to request a claim pack. Or you can visit GOV.UK to download a claim form or make a claim online.

Housing Benefit

Housing Benefit helps pay your rent if you are a tenant on a low income. It will not only reduce your rent but also cover some service charges like lifts and communal laundry facilities. How much you get depends on a number of factors:

- if you rent privately or from a council
- your household income and circumstances
- if you have empty rooms

You may receive more Housing Benefit if you get a disability or carer's benefit, such as Carer's Allowance, Attendance Allowance or Personal Independence Payment.

Housing Benefit is a means-tested benefit. The amount you can claim is affected by: your savings, who you live with, how much rent you pay and how many rooms you have in your home. If you get the Guarantee Credit part of Pension Credit you may get your rent paid in full by Housing Benefit. If you don't get Guarantee Credit - but have a low income and less than £16,000 in savings - you may still get some help.

You can't claim Housing Benefit if you own your own home. However, you may be eligible for Support with Mortgage Interest as part of Pension. If you're not claiming other benefits, you can get a claim form from your local council. You can apply for Housing Benefit at the same time as applying for Pension Credit. If you're already claiming Pension Credit, contact the Pension Service.

Council Tax Support

You may be eligible for Council Tax Support if you're on a low income or claim certain benefits. Council Tax Support replaced Council Tax Benefit in 2013, and each local authority now runs their own Council Tax Support schemes. Apply directly to your local council to see if you're entitled to support.

The support you get may depend on factors such as which benefits you receive, your age, your income, savings, who you live with and how much Council Tax you pay. If you receive a disability or carer's benefit, you may get more Council Tax Support. You may even get your Council Tax paid in full if you get the Guarantee Credit part of Pension Credit. If you don't get Guarantee Credit but have a low income and less than £16,000 in savings, you may still get some help. You can apply whether you own your home, rent, are working or currently unemployed.

Universal Credit

If you're of working age and making a new claim in an area where Universal Credit has been introduced, you should claim Universal Credit to help with your rent. See below for more about Universal Credit.

Pension Credit

Pension Credit is an income-related benefit that comes in two parts and you may be eligible for one or both:

- Guarantee Credit tops up your weekly income to a guaranteed minimum level
- Savings Credit is extra money if you've got some savings or your income is higher than the basic State Pension

About 4 million older people are entitled to Pension Credit, yet about 1 in 3 of those eligible are still not claiming it. Don't be put off if you discover you're only eligible for a small amount of Pension Credit. It's your passport to other benefits, such as Housing Benefit and Council Tax Reduction.

Rates of Pension Credit

Guarantee Credit will top up your weekly income to:

- £163 if you're single
- or £248.80 if you're a couple.

If you qualify for Savings Credit, you can get up to:

- £13.40 extra per week if you're single
- or £14.99 if you're a couple.

Claiming Guarantee Credit

The minimum age to claim Guarantee Credit is gradually rising. From April 2018, it's 65.. If your weekly income is less than £163.00 if you're single, or £248.80 if you're a couple you may qualify for Guarantee Credit. If you have a disability, are a carer or have to pay housing costs, you may be eligible even if your income is higher than the amounts given above.

Claiming Savings Credit

If you're 65 or over you may also qualify for Savings Credit. There isn't a savings limit for Pension Credit, but if you have over £10,000 this will affect the amount you receive. Remember, you can claim one or both parts of Pension Credit.

Benefits of claiming Pension Credit

Pension Credit is also your passport to lots of other savings such as:
- It's unlikely you'll have to pay Council Tax (unless other people live with you).
- You'll get free NHS dental treatment, and you can claim help towards the cost of glasses and travel to hospital.
- You'll get a Cold Weather Payment of £25 when the temperature is 0°C or below for 7 days in a row.
- If you rent your home, you may get your rent paid in full by Housing Benefit.

- If you own your home, you may be eligible for help with mortgage interest, ground rent and service charges.

- If you're a carer, you may get an extra amount known as Carer Premium, or Carer Addition if it's paid with Pension Credit. This is worth up to £34.60 a week.

How make the claim

Call the Pension Credit claim line on 0800 99 1234 (textphone: 0800 169 0133).

Changes to Pension Credit eligibility from 15 May 2019

From 15 May 2019, if you're in a couple you'll only be eligible to start getting pension credit if either:

- you and your partner have both reached Pension Credit qualifying age

- one of you has reached Pension Credit qualifying age and is claiming Housing Benefit (for you as a couple)

If you're not already getting Pension Credit on 14 May 2019, you can backdate your claim. You could still be eligible to get Pension Credit.

You can ask for your claim to be backdated to 14 May or before. You'll need to apply by 13 August 2019 to do this.

You can apply for Universal Credit instead if you're still not eligible.

If you already get Pension Credit and you're in a couple

You'll continue to get Pension Credit after 15 May 2019. If your entitlement stops for any reason, for example your circumstances change, you cannot start getting it again until you (or your partner) are eligible under the new rules.

If you already get Pension Credit and you're single

From 15 May 2019, you'll stop getting Pension Credit if you start living with a partner who is under Pension Credit qualifying age. You can start getting it again when your partner reaches Pension Credit qualifying age.

Savings Credit

You can only start getting Savings Credit if you (and your partner, if you have one) reached State Pension age before 6 April 2016. If your partner did not reach State Pension age before 6 April 2016

If you've been getting Savings Credit since before 6 April 2016, you'll continue to get it as long as there are no breaks in your entitlement.

If you stop being eligible for Savings Credit for any reason, you will not be able to get it again.

Income Support

Income Support is a benefit for people under Pension Credit qualifying age and living on a low income. If you can't work for whatever reason or don't work many hours, you may get some support to top up your income. You can claim Income Support if you're all of the following:

- below the age you can claim Pension Credit
- a carer or, in some cases, if you're sick or disabled, or a single parent with a child under 5

- on a low income and have less than £16,000 in savings
- working fewer than 16 hours a week (if you have a partner they must work fewer than 24 hours a week).

If you qualify for Income Support, you could be entitled to other benefits, such as Housing Benefit or help with Council Tax, health costs or urgent one-off expenses.

Rates of Income support
Rates consist of the following:
- a basic payment (personal allowance)
- extra payments (premiums)

Your income and any savings (over £5,999) can affect how much you get.

Personal allowance
You must be at least 16 to get Income Support.

Status	Age	Weekly payment
Single	16-24	£57.90
Single	25 or over	£73.10
Lone parent	16-17	£57.90
Lone parent	18 and over	£73.10
Couples	Both under 18	£57.90
Couples	Both under 18 Higher rate	£87.50
Couples	One under 18 the other 18-24	£57.90
Couples	One under 18 the other 25 or over	£73.10

129

Couples	One under 18 one over higher rate	£114.85
Couples	both 18 or over	£114.85

Higher rate

You could get the higher rate if either of you is responsible for a child, or if each of you would be eligible for one of the following if you were not a couple:

- Employment and Support Allowance
- Income Support
- Jobseeker's Allowance

Premiums

You could also get an Income Support 'premium' - this is extra money based on your circumstances, for example if:

- your partner is a pensioner
- you're disabled or a carer

The benefit cap

The benefit cap limits the total amount of benefit you can get. It applies to most people aged 16 or over who have not reached State pension Age. Some individual benefits are not affected, but it may affect the total amount of benefit you get.

You can claim Income Support by phone. Contact Jobcentre Plus on 0800 169 0130 or textphone 0800 023 4888. Or you can you can fill out a claim form on GOV.UK. Print it out and post it to your local Jobcentre.

Jobseeker's Allowance

You might be able to get Jobseeker's Allowance (JSA) while you look for a full-time job. You can get it while you're out of work, or if you're working less than 16 hours a week.

There are 2 types of JSA:

- income-based
- contribution-based - this is also called 'new style' JSA if you're getting Universal Credit or you're in a Universal Credit full service area

Both pay the same personal allowance, but the application process is different. Use this page to check if you can get JSA, and which type you need to claim.

You can usually claim either type of JSA if you're under State Pension age and are:

- not working full-time (less than 16 hours a week)
- available to work full-time
- actively looking for full-time work
- not in full-time education

not claiming Income Support

Your wages will affect your JSA claim, and the rules are complicated.

Check if you can get contribution-based or 'new style' JSA

It's best to claim contribution-based JSA if you can. This is because your savings, capital, and partner's income won't affect your claim. You can usually get contribution-based JSA for 6 months if you:

- meet the basic conditions
- have worked and paid National Insurance during the last 2 years

- haven't claimed contribution-based JSA in the last 2 years

Before you apply, check if you're eligible for Universal Credit - if you are, you'll need to apply for 'new style JSA' instead.

When you put in your postcode, make a note of whether you're in a 'live' or 'full' service area - you'll be asked this when you apply.

New-style JSA pays the same as contribution-based JSA, but the application process is different.

If you can't get contribution-based JSA

You should still check if you're eligible for Universal Credit - if you are, you'll need to apply for that instead. It pays the same as JSA, but the application process is different.

If you aren't eligible for Universal Credit, and have claimed contribution-based JSA in the past 2 years, you'll usually need to claim 'income-based JSA'. You can normally get it as long as you:

- meet the basic conditions
- have less than £16,000 in capital

aren't claiming Income Support, income-related ESA or Pension Credit

Capital generally includes savings and one-off payments like inheritance, redundancy payouts or winnings from premium bonds. It doesn't include your home, personal possessions or your pension.

How much JSA you'll get

Each type of JSA pays the same 'personal allowance' each week - if you're eligible, you can get up to:

132

- £57.90 if you're 18 to 24
- £73.10 if you're 25 or over
- £114.85 if you claim income-related JSA as a couple

The exact amount you get will depend on your circumstances - for example, if you work part-time your payment might be less.

You can get extra payments on top of your personal allowance in some cases - these are called 'premiums'. You get a premium if you claim income-based JSA and you or your partner are:

- disabled
- a carer getting Carer's Allowance
- over the State Pension age for a woman

You need to claim income-based JSA to get these premiums - you can claim both types of JSA if you need to. You'll only get one personal allowance, but you'll get the premiums you're entitled to as part of income-based JSA.

Getting help with housing costs

If you claim income-based JSA, you might get extra payments to help with your housing costs - these are usually paid straight to your landlord, lender or mortgage provider. As with the additional 'premiums', you'll need to claim income-based JSA to get help with housing costs. You can claim both contribution-based and income-based JSA at the same time.

You need to ask for help with housing costs if you apply for JSA over the phone. If you apply online, it'll be on the first section of the claim form.

If you rent your home

You might qualify for Housing Benefit to help pay rent while you claim income-based JSA.

If you have a mortgage or other loan for your home

You might be able to get a government loan to help pay the interest on a mortgage, or another loan to pay for things like:

- the freehold of your property
- your ex-partner's share in your property
- major repairs and improvements

The loan is called 'support for mortgage interest (SMI). You'll need to pay it back - but only when you sell your home or give it to someone else.

SMI is usually paid directly to your mortgage or loan provider. It only helps pay the interest on what you've borrowed, not the repayments.

SMI will usually start 39 weeks (about 9 months) after you claim JSA.

If the DWP think you can get SMI, they'll ask if you want to apply for it. They'll usually ask 7 or 8 months after you claim JSA.

If you pay ground rent or service charge

You can get an additional JSA payment to help with your ground rent if your lease has more than 21 years left. You won't have to pay this money back.

You might also be able to get help paying service charges if they're for:

- building insurance - if it's part of a condition of your lease
- small repairs, for example to water pipes or heating
- small improvements, for example painting a hallway

You can't get normally help with your service charge if it's for major improvements or repairs, but there are some exceptions - for example if your home would've been unsafe without structural repairs.

It can take up to 39 weeks to get these expenses included in your income-based JSA claim, so it's best to apply for them as soon as possible.

Employment and Support Allowance

Employment and Support Allowance (ESA) is a benefit for people who are unable to work due to illness or disability. There are 2 types of ESA, and you may be entitled to one or both of them:

- Contribution-based ESA - you can get this if you've paid enough National Insurance contributions. It's taxable.
- Income-related ESA - you can get this if you have no income or a low income. You don't have to have paid National Insurance contributions and it isn't taxable.

During your claim you'll be called to 2 compulsory reviews, one after 13 weeks and the other after 26 weeks. You can't claim income-related ESA if you claim Universal Credit or have savings of more than £16,000.

You'll have to attend a medical assessment called a 'work capability assessment'. You'll also have to fill in a 'limited capacity for work' questionnaire that looks at how your illness or disability affects what you do. After this you'll be told whether you're considered fit for work, or whether you're entitled to ESA.

If you are entitled to ESA, you'll be placed in the 'work-related activity group' or the 'support group'. People in the support group are exempt from the benefit cap. People in the work-related activity group get less money and are expected to prepare for an eventual return to the job market. If you don't, your benefit can be reduced for a period.

If you're entitled to income-related ESA, you may also qualify for other benefits such as Housing Benefit, Council Tax Reduction and help with health costs.

Rates of ESA

You'll normally get the assessment rate for 13 weeks after your claim. This will be:

- up to £57.90 a week if you're aged under 25
- up to £73.10 a week if you're aged 25 or over

After that, if you're entitled to ESA, you'll be placed in one of 2 groups and will receive:

- up to £73.10 a week if you're in the work-related activity group
- up to £110.75 a week if you're in the support group

You might get more ESA in the work-related activity group if you applied before 3 April 2017.

If you're in the support group and on income-related ESA, you're also entitled to the enhanced disability premium at £16.40 or £23.55 a week.

You may also qualify for the severe disability premium at £64.30 or £128.60 a week.

If the assessment takes longer than 13 weeks your benefit will be backdated to the 14th week of the claim.

Work-related support

Following your Work Capability Assessment you'll be placed in either the work-related activity group or support group if you're entitled to ESA.

Work-related activity group

You must go to regular interviews with an adviser who can help with things like job goals and improving your skills.

Support group

You do not have to go to interviews, but you can ask to talk to a personal adviser. You're usually in this group if your illness or disability severely limits what you can do.

How long you'll get ESA for

'New style' and contribution-based ESA last for 365 days if you're in the work-related activity group.

There's no time limit if you're in the support group, or if you're getting income-based ESA.

Benefits sanctions

Your ESA can be reduced if you do not go to interviews or do work-related activity as agreed with your adviser. This reduction can continue for up to 4 weeks after you restart the interviews or activity.

You'll get a 'sanction letter'. Tell your ESA adviser if you have a good reason for missing the interview.

You'll get another letter if the decision is made to give you a sanction. Your benefit will only be affected once a decision has been made.

You should contact your local council immediately if you claim Housing Benefit or Council Tax Reduction. They'll tell you what to do to continue getting support.

If you get a sanction you can:
• ask for the decision to be looked at again
• ask for a 'hardship payment'
• You will not get a sanction if you're in the support group.
• Hardship payments
You may be able to get a hardship payment if your income-related ESA has been reduced because of a sanction or fraud penalty. You do not have to pay it back.

A hardship payment is a reduced amount of your ESA (usually 60% or 80% of the basic rate, depending on your circumstances).

Eligibility

You can get a hardship payment if you cannot pay for rent, heating, food or other basic needs for you or your family.

You must be 18 or over.

How to claim

Speak to your Jobcentre Plus adviser or work coach to find out how to claim a hardship payment.

Jobcentre Plus

Telephone: 0800 169 0310

Universal credit

Universal Credit is a payment to help with living costs. It's paid monthly - or twice a month for some people in Scotland. You may be able to get it if you're on a low income or out of work

The roll out of universal credit has been delayed and restricted due to complications arising from the implementation. the following are the basic facts.

If you already get benefits

Universal Credit will replace the following benefits:

- Child Tax Credit
- Housing Benefit
- Income Support

- income-based Jobseeker's Allowance (JSA)
- income-related Employment and Support Allowance (ESA)
- Working Tax Credit

If you currently receive any of these benefits, you cannot claim Universal Credit at the same time.

Universal Credit is being introduced in stages across the UK. You do not need to do anything until you hear from the Department for Work and Pensions (DWP) about moving to Universal Credit, unless you have a change in circumstances.

Severe disability premium

You cannot claim Universal Credit if you either:

- are getting the Severe Disability Premium
- got the severe disability premium within the last month and you're still eligible for it

You may be able to get Universal Credit if:

- you're on a low income or out of work
- you're 18 or over (there are some exceptions if you're 16 to 17)
- you're under State Pension Credit qualifying age (or your partner is)
- you and your partner have £16,000 or less in savings between you
- you live in the UK

The number of children you have does not affect your eligibility for Universal Credit, but it may affect how much you get.

If you live with your partner

Your partner's income and savings will be taken into account, even if they are not eligible for Universal Credit.

If you're 16 or 17

You can make a new Universal Credit claim if any of the following apply:

- you have limited capability for work or you have medical evidence and are waiting for a Work Capability Assessment
- you're caring for a severely disabled person
- you're responsible for a child
- you're in a couple with responsibility for at least one child and your partner is eligible for Universal Credit
- you're pregnant and it's 11 weeks or less before your expected week of childbirth
- you've had a child in the last 15 weeks
- you do not have parental support, for example you're estranged from your parents and you're not under local authority care

If you're in training or studying full-time

You can make a new Universal Credit claim if any of the following apply:

- you live with your partner and they're eligible for Universal Credit
- you're responsible for a child, either as a single person or as a couple
- you're disabled and entitled to Disability Living Allowance (DLA) or Personal Independence Payment (PIP) and have limited capability for work

- you're in 'non-advanced education' (for example studying for A levels or a BTEC National Diploma), are 21 or under and do not have parental support

If you've reached Pension Credit qualifying age

You can only claim if you live with a partner who is eligible for Universal Credit and under Pension Credit qualifying age - you'll have to make a joint claim. If you prefer, you can make a claim for Pension Credit as a couple instead.

Caps on all benefits

The government has imposed a cap on the amount of benfits an inividual or couple/family can receive over the course of a year. The cap applies to the total amount that the people in your household get from the following benefits:

- Bereavement Allowance
- Child Benefit
- Child Tax Credit
- Employment and Support Allowance
- Housing Benefit
- Incapacity Benefit
- Income Support
- Jobseeker's Allowance
- Maternity Allowance
- Severe Disablement Allowance
- Widowed Parent's Allowance (or Widowed Mother's Allowance or Widow's Pension if you started getting it before 9 April 2001)
- Universal Credit

The level of the cap is:

- £500 a week for couples (with or without children living with them)
- £500 a week for single parents whose children live with them
- £350 a week for single adults who don't have children, or whose children don't live with them

This may mean the amount you get for certain benefits will go down to make sure that the total amount you get isn't more than the cap level.

Who won't be affected?

You might still be affected by the cap if you have any grown-up children or non-dependants who live with you and they qualify for one of the benefits below. This is because they won't normally count as part of your household.

You're not affected by the benefit cap if anyone in your household qualifies for Working Tax Credit or gets any of the following benefits: You're not affected by the cap if you or your partner:

- get Working Tax Credit (even if the amount you get is £0)
- are over State Pension age
- get Universal Credit because of a disability or health condition that stops you from working (this is called 'limited capability for work and work-related activity')
- get Universal Credit because you care for someone with a disability

143

- get Universal Credit and you and your partner earn more than £542 a month combined, after tax and National Insurance contributions

You're also not affected by the cap if you, your partner or any children under 18 living with you gets:
- Armed Forces Compensation Scheme
- Armed Forces Independence Payment
- Attendance Allowance
- Carer's Allowance
- Disability Living Allowance (DLA)
- Employment and Support Allowance (if you get the support component)
- Guardian's Allowance
- Industrial Injuries Benefits (and equivalent payments as part of a War Disablement Pension or the Armed Forces Compensation Scheme)
- Personal Independence Payment (PIP)
- War pensions
- War Widow's or War Widower's Pension

The amount you get through the benefit cap depends on whether:
- you live inside or outside Greater London
- you're single or in a couple
- your children live with you (if you're single)

If you're in a couple but you do not live together, you'll get the amounts for a single person.

Outside Greater London

The benefit cap outside Greater London is:

- £384.62 per week (£20,000 a year) if you're in a couple
- £384.62 per week (£20,000 a year) if you're a single parent and your children live with you
- £257.69 per week (£13,400 a year) if you're a single adult

Inside Greater London

The benefit cap inside Greater London is:

- £442.31 per week (£23,000 a year) if you're in a couple
- £442.31 per week (£23,000 a year) if you're a single parent and your children live with you
- £296.35 per week (£15,410 a year) if you're a single adult

Working Tax credits

Universal Credit and Working Tax Credit

Most people will not be able to make a new claim for Working Tax Credit and will be asked to apply for Universal Credit. If you're already claiming Working Tax Credit, you will have to move to Universal Credit before March 2023. How and when you move depends on if you have to make a new claim because of a change in circumstances, or are asked to claim Universal Credit by the Department for Work and Pensions (DWP).

What is working tax credit?

Working Tax Credit is designed to top up your earnings if you work and you're on a low income. If you're eligible, you can get it if you're employed or self-employed.

You will get a basic element of £1,960 a year plus extra elements, depending on your circumstances, such as having a disability or paying for childcare.

You can't claim Working Tax Credit if you already get Universal Credit.

Do I qualify for Working Tax Credit?

You can usually only make a new claim for Working Tax Credit if:

- you or your partner qualify for Pension Credit.

Depending on your circumstances, you might be able to claim Working Tax Credit if:

- you're aged between 16 and 24 and have a child or a disability, or
- you're 25 or over and working a minimum number of hours.

Your circumstance	Minimum number of working hours a week
Aged 25 to 59	30
Aged 60+	16
Disabled	16
Single with one or more children	16
Couple with one or more children	Usually at least 24 hours between you (with one of you working at least 16 hours)

Exceptions for couples with at least one child

You can claim if you work less than 24 hours a week between you and one of the following applies:

- you work at least 16 hours a week and you're disabled or aged 60 or above

- you work at least 16 hours a week and your partner is getting certain benefits because of disability or ill health, is entitled to Carer's Allowance, or is in hospital or prison.

Annual household income limits

Tax credits are tax-free and you don't have to be paying National Insurance or tax to qualify. When you apply, the Tax Credit Office will take into account your circumstances (and those of your partner or spouse) when deciding how much you're entitled to. If your annual household income is £6,420 or below, you'll get the maximum amount for each Working Tax Credit element you qualify for. This is called the 'income threshold' - anything you earn above this will reduce the amount you can get.

If you or your partner earns over a certain amount, you won't be entitled to Working Tax Credit. This is called the annual household income limit. The table below gives you a rough idea of the income limits for getting Working Tax Credit if you:

- are over 25
- don't have a disability
- don't have any children.

Number of children	Annual household income limit 2018-19
None - single person	Around £13,100
None - couple	around £18,000

147

There are different income limits depending on your circumstances, for example, if you or your partner have a disability, or you have children.

If you have dependent children, your annual household income limits might be higher and you might be entitled to Child Tax Credit.

How much is Working Tax Credit?

If you're eligible, you'll get a basic amount of £1,960 a year (known as the 'basic element'). You'll get extra amounts ('elements') on top of this, depending on your circumstances. The amount you get for each element depends on things like:

- your income
- how many hours you work
- whether you have a disability
- whether you have children
- whether you pay for childcare.

The rates for the 2018 to 2019 tax year

Element	Yearly amount
For a couple applying together or a single parent (the 'couples and lone parent element')	Up to £2,010
If you work at least 30 hours a week (the '30 hour element')	Up to £810
If you work and are disabled (the 'disability element')	Up to £3,090
If you're severely disabled (the 'severe disability element')	Up to £1,330

Element	Yearly amount
If you're paying for registered or approved childcare (the 'childcare element')	Up to 70% of your childcare costs

Working Tax Credit and help with childcare costs

If you work at least 16 hours a week and pay for childcare, you might be able to claim the 'childcare element' of Working Tax Credit to help with up to 70% of your childcare costs:

- if you're in a couple, you need to be working at least 16 hours each to qualify

- you can be eligible if you're employed or self-employed

In most cases, you must use registered or approved childcare. This can include childminders, playgroups and nurseries.

How much can you get?

With the childcare element, you can get help with up to 70% of your childcare costs, up to certain maximum weekly limits. The table below shows how much you could get in the 2018-19 tax year:

Number of children	If you pay up to:	You could get up to:
1	£175 a week	£122.50 a week
2 or more	£300 a week	£210 a week

If you pay more than this for childcare, you will still only receive the maximum amount shown above. If you qualify for the childcare element, you won't necessarily get the full amounts.

How much you get will depend on:

- your income

- the hours you work

149

- your childcare costs.

Leave, sickness and gaps in your employment

If you're eligible, you can get Working Tax Credit for periods when you're not working. For example, if you're sick, on maternity leave or you've lost your job. Depending on the circumstances, you can claim Working Tax Credit for a set period of time, if you qualify. To qualify, you must:

- have been in paid work
- have worked the right number of hours before you went on leave or the gap happened
- have got Statutory Sick Pay or an equivalent benefit if you were on sick leave.

Circumstance	Period you get tax credits for
You lose or leave your job	4 weeks
You're on maternity leave or adoption leave	The first 39 weeks of your leave
You're on paternity leave	The period of your ordinary paternity leave
You're on additional paternity leave	Up to the equivalent 39th week of your partner's leave
You're off sick	The first 28 weeks
You're on strike	The first 10 days
You're laid off work	4 weeks
You're suspended from work - for example, because of a complaint	Usually the period of the suspension

If you don't return to work at the end of this time off, call the Tax Credits Helpline on 0345 300 3900 and let them know.

How to claim Working Tax Credit

Call the Tax Credits Helpline:

- Telephone: 0345 300 3900
- Textphone: 0345 300 3909
- Outside UK: +44 2890 538 192
- Opening times: 8am to 8pm, Monday to Friday, 8am to 4pm Saturday, 9am to 5pm Sunday

Keeping your tax credits up to date

You need to renew your tax credits claim every year if you want to keep getting them. The Tax Credits Office will write to you to telling you what you need to do to renew your tax credits. If your circumstances change at any time during the year (for example, if your income changes, your child leaves home or you move house), you should call the Tax Credit Office on 0345 300 3900 to let them know.

Changes in your circumstances can affect the amount of money you get, or mean you have to make a new claim for Universal Credit.

Tax credits and income changes

A significant income change might count as a change in circumstances, which would mean you will have to make a new claim for Universal Credit instead of tax credits. The amount by which your income can change before you have to tell the Tax Credit Office is £2,500. This is called the income disregard.

If your income goes up

If your income goes up by £2,500 or more and you delay telling the Tax Credit Office or wait until the next time your claim is due to be re-assessed, you might find you have been overpaid tax credits.

You'll be asked to pay this extra money back, either by reducing your future tax credits or by direct payments if your tax credits have stopped. To avoid a bill, it's even more important to tell the Tax Credit Office within 30 days of when you get the extra money. It'll be easier for your tax credits to be adjusted, and decrease the chance you'll be chased for overpayments at a later date.

If your income goes down

If your income falls by £2,500 or more, you might be entitled to more tax credits, or be asked to claim Universal Credit. Tell the Tax Credit Office as soon as possible about your change of circumstances.

Other tax credits you might qualify for

If you qualify for Working Tax Credit, have children and are on a low income, you might also be eligible for Child Tax Credit. When you apply for Working Tax Credit, you'll also be told whether you qualify for Child Tax Credi

Winter fuel payments

Winter Fuel Payment or Winter Fuel Allowance is an annual payment to help with heating costs, made to households with someone over Pension Credit age. Not heating homes properly puts people at risk of cold-related illnesses such as a heart attack or even hypothermia. The rates for winter fuel payment currently are £200 if you're under 80 and £300 if you're 80 or over

You will qualify for the payment if you were born before 5 January 1953.

You only need to claim once. After this, you should get it automatically each year, as long as your circumstances do not change. The payment is made directly into your bank account in November or December. For more information you should call the Winter Fuel Payments Helpline on 0800 731 0160.

Cold Weather Payment

Cold Weather Payments are made to eligible people when the weather is very cold. You get £25 a week when the average temperature has been, or is expected to be, 0°C or below for 7 days in a row (between 1 November and 31 March).

You automatically receive the payment, if you get Pension Credit or certain other means-tested benefits. If you think that you are entitled to a cold weather payment and don't get one contact the Pension Service.

TV licence concessions

You could be entitled to a concession for a TV licence if you are over 75 or someone who is over 75 lives with you. You could also be entitled if you are registered as blind or severely sight impaired or are retired or disabled and live in certain accommodation

The TV licence for your main home doesn't cover you if you have a second home. You will have to buy a separate licence. If you have a licence for your main home, you won't need another if you have a static caravan or mobile home and you don't use the TV at the same time in both places.

You need to apply for a free TV licence if you're 75 or over as it's not given out automatically. You'll need to provide your date of birth and National insurance number (or a photocopy of your passport, driving licence or birth certificate). If you share your house with someone younger than 75, you can still apply for a free licence but it must be in your name. You can apply for your concession by calling 0300 790 6165 or visiting the TV licensing website. Once you have your free TV licence, it will renew automatically annually.

If you apply for a TV licence and you are 74 when you renew your licence you can apply for a short term licence until you are 75.

Concessions for blind and sight-impaired

If you're blind or severely sight-impaired, you can claim a 50% discount on your TV licence. When you apply, you'll need to provide a photocopy of the certificate from your local authority or ophthalmologist confirming your status as well as your TV licence application form and fee. Once you're registered, all your TV licence renewals will be at the concessionary rate.

If you live with someone who is blind or severely-sight impaired, you can get the 50% discount if you transfer the TV licence to the name of that person. You can apply for your concession by calling 0300 790 6165 or visiting the TV licensing website. If you've already paid the TV licence fee but qualify for the blind concession, fill out the TV Licensing online refund form.

Care homes and sheltered housing

You may be entitled to a TV licence concession if you live in a care home or sheltered housing. This licence is called an Accommodation for Residential Care (ARC) licence and it costs £7.50. You'll only need to get one if you watch TV in your own separate accommodation, not if you only watch it in common areas such as a residents' lounge. To qualify, you must be retired and aged 60 or over or disabled and live in accommodation which is eligible. If you think you qualify, contact the warden, staff or managing authority where you live. They will apply for one for you.

If you've already paid your full licence fee and now qualify for an ARC licence, ask your care home manager to help you apply for a refund. If you have questions about the ARC licence, phone TV licensing on 0300 790 6011 or visit the TV licensing website.

Bereavement allowance

You may be able to get a £2,000 Bereavement Payment if your spouse or civil partner died before 6 April 2017. This is a one-off, tax-free, lump-sum payment.

If your spouse or civil partner died on or after 6 April 2017 you may be eligible for Bereavement Support Payment instead.

You may be able to get Bereavement Payment if, when your husband, wife or civil partner died, you were either:

- under State Pension age
- over State Pension age and your husband, wife or civil partner wasn't entitled to a State Pension based on their own national insurance contributions

Additionally, your husband, wife or civil partner must have either:

- paid enough National Insurance contributions
- died because of an industrial accident or disease

When you can't get Bereavement Payment

You can't get Bereavement Payment if any of the following are true:

- you were divorced from your husband, wife or civil partner

- you're living with another person as husband, wife or civil partner
- you're in prison

Other bereavement benefits

You may also be eligible for:

- Widowed parents Allowance- if you're bringing up children
- Bereavement Allowance

You don't have to apply more than once - you'll be considered for all bereavement benefits when you apply for one.

If you're abroad

If you've moved abroad contact the International Pension Centre to find out if you can claim.

Bereavement and widows' benefits if you're abroad

Telephone: +44 191 21 87608
Department for Work and Pensions Bereavement and widows' benefits International Pension Centre Tyneview Park Newcastle-upon-Tyne
NE98 1BA

Bereavement Support payment

You may be able to get Bereavement Support Payment if your husband, wife or civil partner died on or after 6 April 2017. You could be eligible if your partner either:

- paid National Insurance contributions for at least 25 weeks
- died because of an accident at work or a disease caused by work

When they died you must have been:

- under State Pension age
- living in the UK or a country that pays bereavement benefits

You cannot claim Bereavement Support Payment if you're in prison.

You'll get a first payment and then up to 18 monthly payments. There are 2 rates.

Rate	First payment	Monthly payment
Higher rate	£3500	£350
Lower rate	£2500	£100

If you get Child Benefit (or if you do not get it but are entitled to it), you'll get the higher rate. If you do not get Child Benefit, you'll get the lower rate unless you were pregnant when your husband, wife or civil partner died.

You must claim within 3 months of your husband, wife or civil partner's death to get the full amount. You can claim up to 21 months after but your payments will be less.

Widowed Parent's Allowance

You may get Widowed Parent's Allowance (WPA) if all the following apply:

- your husband, wife or civil partner died before 6 April 2017 (if your spouse or partner died after this date then you might be able to get bereavement support instead)
- you're under State Pension age
- you're entitled to Child Benefit for at least one child and your late husband, wife or civil partner was their parent

- your late husband, wife or civil partner paid National Insurance contributions, or they died as a result of an industrial accident or disease

You may also claim WPA if you're pregnant and your husband has died, or you're pregnant after fertility treatment and your civil partner has died.

If your husband, wife or civil partner died on or after 6 April 2017 you may be eligible for Bereavement Support Payment instead. You cannot claim WPA if you:

- were divorced from your husband, wife or civil partner when they died
- remarry or are living with another person as if you're married to them or as if you've formed a civil partnership
- were over State Pension age when you were widowed or became a surviving civil partner – you may be able to get extra State Pension
- are in prison

What you'll get

The amount you get is based on how much your late husband, wife or civil partner paid in National Insurance contributions. The maximum Widowed Parent's Allowance (WPA) is £117.10 a week.

If your husband, wife or civil partner died as a result of an industrial accident or disease, you may claim WPA even if they did not pay National Insurance contributions. You can get WPA until you stop being entitled to Child Benefit, unless you reach State Pension age first.

If your WPA ends within 52 weeks of your husband, wife or civil partner's death, you may be able to get Bereavement Allowance for the rest of the 52 weeks.

Effect on other benefits

Once you get WPA, payments may change if you're getting any of the following:

- Income support
- Incapacity Benefit
- Jobseeker's Allowance
- Carer's Allowance
- Employment and Support Allowance
- Universal Credit

Widow's pension

The widow's pension, awarded to widows over age 45, was replaced by the bereavement allowance in 2001. The bereavement allowance is given to widows, widowers or surviving civil partners over age 45 until they reach state pension age. It is paid for up to 52 weeks.

This benefit only applies to people whose partner's died before 6 April 2017. If they died on or after this date, they could qualify for bereavement support payment. The amount you'll get depends on your age at the time of your partner's death, and the overall level of their National Insurance contributions, as the table below shows.

It also depends on your age when your partner dies. The younger you are, the less you'll get. The rates in 2018/19 are as follows: earnings.

AGE WHEN SPOUSE DIES	WEEKLY ALLOWANCE
45	£35.13
46	£45.33
47	£51.52
48	£59.72
49	£67.92
50	£76.12
51	£84.31
52	£92.51
53	£100.71
54	£108.90
55 UNTIL STATE PENSION AGE	£117.10

Am I eligible for bereavement allowance?

These are the criteria for claiming bereavement allowance:

- You were aged 45 or over when your partner died.
- You're under state pension age.
- Your partner paid National Insurance contributions, or died in an industrial accident or disease
- You aren't raising children.
- You haven't remarried/joined a civil partnership.
- You aren't living with another person as if you're married/in a civil partnership with them.
- You're not in prison.

Payments for funeral expenses

If you have to pay for a funeral for your partner, a close relative or friend, you may be able to claim a funeral payment from the Social Fund. Partners include lesbian, gay and heterosexual partners, whether you were married, in a civil partnership or living together. To get a funeral payment, you must be getting Income Support, income-based Jobseeker's Allowance, income-related Employment and Support Allowance, Pension Credit, Universal Credit or Housing Benefit. Some people getting Child Tax Credit or Working Tax Credit may also be entitled to a funeral payment.

Financial help if your husband, wife or civil partner was in the Armed Forces

If your husband, wife or civil partner died as a result of serving in the Armed Forces, you may be able to get financial help from the Service Personnel and Veterans Agency (SPVA). It does not matter whether your husband, wife or civil partner died during active service or not, as long as the death was caused by service in the Armed Forces. You may get a War Widow's or War Widower's pension, or a guaranteed income payment (based on your spouse or civil partner's earnings), depending on when the injury, illness or death was caused.

******

www.straightforwardco.co.uk

All titles, listed below, in the Straightforward Guides Series can be purchased online, using credit card or other forms of payment by going to www.straightfowardco.co.uk A discount of 25% per title is offered with online purchases.

Law
A Straightforward Guide to:

Consumer Rights

Bankruptcy Insolvency and the Law

Employment Law

Private Tenants Rights

Family law

Small Claims in the County Court

Contract law

Intellectual Property and the law

Divorce and the law

Leaseholders Rights

The Process of Conveyancing

Knowing Your Rights and Using the Courts

Producing Your own Will

Housing Rights

The Bailiff the law and You

Probate and The Law

Company law

What to Expect When You Go to Court

Give me Your Money-Guide to Effective Debt Collection

Rights of Disabled people

General titles

Letting Property for Profit

Buying, Selling and Renting property

Buying a Home in England and France

Buying and Selling a Property Abroad

Bookkeeping and Accounts for Small Business

Creative Writing

Freelance Writing

Writing Your own Life Story

Writing Performance Poetry

Writing Romantic Fiction

Essay Writing

Speech Writing

Teaching Your Child to Read and write

Creating a Successful Commercial Website

The Straightforward Business Plan

The Straightforward C.V.

Successful Public Speaking

Handling Bereavement

Play the Game-A Compendium of Rules

Individual and Personal Finance

Understanding Mental Illness

The Two Minute Message

Guide to Self Defence

Buying and Selling on Auction Sites

Buying and Selling a Property at Auction

Go to: www.straightforwardco.co.uk